# THE EVOLUTION OF BREATH

Explore the Fascinating History & Hidden Secrets of Breathing, Reveal the Scientific Discoveries & Key Evolutionary Milestones, and Uncover its Powerful Impact on Human Biology

## SOWMIYA SREE

# YOUR FREE GIFT !!

As a token of my thanks for taking out time to read my book, I would like to offer you a **Free-Gift**:

Click Below and Download your free checklist:

**"Daily Breathing Habits for Better Health"**

You can also grab your **FREE GIFT** by typing in the below URL:
**https://sowmiya-sree.ck.page/**

# About the Author

S owmiya Sree is a passionate reader and a gold medalist post-graduate in Pharmacognosy, having received the honor from the late former President of India, **Dr. APJ Abdul Kalam**. She explores diverse health and personal growth topics, and human anatomy fascinates her.

As a yoga practitioner, Sowmiya believes in the true potential of breath and its marvelous effects on our bodies, and she savors its benefits. With a deep curiosity about the impact of breathing in the world around her and within her, Sowmiya attempts to correlate her academic knowledge with her passion for storytelling to create a better world.

Connect author at: www.sowmiyasree.com

# ACKNOWLEDGMENT

My journey as a writer is unexpected, not only for me, but also for those around me. My mom, Sunitha, and dad, Rajendran, were not astonished by my new passion. Their unwavering belief in me, a belief I cannot fully comprehend, has been the cornerstone of my writing journey. Your confidence in me has given me the inner strength to write this book. None of it exists without you both, me, or my book.

Ezhil, my dear husband, without you, I would have finished this work two months earlier. But the truth is, without your love, I am incomplete and incompetent. Thanks for being my partner; your presence always uplifts my spirits, which gave me the peace of mind to write this book.

My daughter Swasthika and my son Ahir Krishna, you are my world. Your curiosity about my work has compelled me to finish this book, and your constant questioning has boosted this creation.

The most challenging part of producing this book was finding the time. This precious resource was made more available to me thanks to the selfless support of my mother-in-law, Maheswari. She shouldered my responsibilities, allowing me the time and space to focus on my writing. I am deeply grateful for her love.

Thanks to the researchers, I am astonished by the wealth of knowledge surrounding us. I included all your contributions in my reference pages. Without the depth of research that went into it, this book is not complete.

This journey helped me find my passion, quenching my thirst for science. Thanks to my teachers, who molded me into who I am. Thanks to Som Bathla, my mentor, who guided me throughout this journey. Also, thanks for your knowledge and suggestions in the hot seat audit. A teacher will appear when a student is ready; true to this, you appeared before me.

Thanks to Sooraj Achar for your patience. You have always delivered more than I expected. Thanks for hand-holding me towards the unknown path of this publishing world. Thanks to everyone on your team who helped me so much. Special thanks to the Iconic Agency, my cover designer, and Sooraj Achar for formatting, editing, and proofreading my manuscript.

*To my mother-in-law: If time is the most precious gift,*
*then without you, I wouldn't be able to finish this book.*

"Then the LORD God
formed the man of dust from
the ground and breathed into
his nostrils the breath of life,
and the man became a living
being."

-GENESIS 2:7

# CONTENTS

# TIMELINE OF BREATH

**4.3 Billion Years Ago: Origin of life**

- Anaerobic Respiration: Early bacteria survive without oxygen.

**2.4 Billion Years Ago: The Great Oxidation Event**

-Oxygen Production: Cyanobacteria start producing oxygen through photosynthesis.

**2.3 Billion Years Ago: Aerobic Respiration**

-Oxygen Breathing. Organisms learn to use oxygen for energy, leading to more complex life forms.

**525 Million Years Ago: Filter Feeding**

- Cephalochordate, was mastering the art of filter feeding.

**500 Million Years Ago: Development of Gills.**

-Fish developed Gills for extracting oxygen from water.

## 470 Million Years Ago: Land Plants Emerge

-Oxygen Increases: Land plants boost atmospheric oxygen, supporting diverse life on Earth.

## 400 Million Years Ago: Fish Develop Lungs

- Transition to Land: Fish evolve primitive lungs, a step towards land-dwelling animals.

## 375 Million Years Ago: First Land Vertebrates

-Lungs and Limbs: Early amphibians use lungs to breathe air.

## 150 Million Years Ago: Birds Evolve

-One-Way Breathing: Birds develop a unique respiratory system for flight.

## 200,000 Years Ago: Homo sapiens

-Human Respiration: Modern humans develop a highly efficient respiratory system.

# PART-1

MIGHTY OCEAN

# Chapter 1

# GENESIS

*"One of the most significant events in our distant past
is still perhaps the greatest mystery: the origins of life
itself." ~* Neil deGrasse Tyson

As Mr. Neil said, genesis is one of the greatest mysteries humanity has been trying to solve for thousands of years. Although many hypotheses and mythology are available, a solid theory has yet to be established. Each religion in the world tried to answer the question. Science, too, worked hard to solve the puzzle. But the mystery continues: how, when, where, and what happened?

The story of the universe is as old as time itself. 13.7 billion years ago, dense, compact, hot matter exploded in an event known as the Big Bang. This event gave birth to a young, hot, and denser universe—too hot even for atoms to exist. As the universe expanded, its temperature and density decreased. Atoms formed first, then molecules. Gravity drew matter together to form clusters, eventually bringing the stars, planets, and galaxies into existence. The universe formed in this high-energy event gradually cooled to create the great cosmos.

About 4.6 billion years ago, the Sun formed from a spinning cloud of gas and dust called the solar nebula. As the nebula collapsed under its gravity, it spun faster and flattened into a disk, forming the golden sphere.

Within a billion years of the sun's appearance, Earth took shape approximately 4.5 billion years ago, a celestial body pulled together by gravity from the remnants of the solar nebula. Our sweet home, this third planet from the Sun, began its journey.

## ORIGIN OF LIFE

When did life begin? There is no precise answer, but it began approximately 4.3 billion years ago, during the Hadean eon. The oldest known fossil evidence of life is stromatolite. These mat-like sedimentary structures formed by colonies of microorganisms compressed into stone are found in rocks in western Greenland, which is 3.7 billion years old.

Where did life originate? There are many theories. Still, the most widely accepted theory points to deep alkaline hydrothermal vents like black smokers and the lost city situated in the lap of the Hadean ocean. Some of the world's oldest fossils are obtained from these vents to support this idea. This is not a fantasy story, but the tale of our existence.

Life emerged in a bleak and fiery world in a chaotic condition inside deep-sea vents. When seawater oozed into the newly formed rocks in the upper mantle of the earth's crust, it reacted with the minerals in the rocks, like iron, producing alkaline fluids rich in hydrogen, sulfide, and other minerals like nickel, zinc, cobalt, etc. These fluids typically have high pH values and are alkaline, whereas primordial seawater is acidic and rich in iron and carbon dioxide.

How did life originate? Iron-sulfur biofilms were precipitated when these alkaline fluids met acidic seawater. Inside these compartments, the vents' hydrogen and the seawater's carbon dioxide react to form simple organic compounds like methane, formate, and acetate. The iron-sulfur biofilm itself acts as a catalyst for this reaction.

The electrochemical gradient between the vent and seawater forms acetyl phosphate and pyrophosphate, similar to today's adenosine 5'-triphosphate (ATP). These molecules lead to the formation of amino acids, giving rise to nucleotides. Hydrogen and carbon dioxide diffusion, along with thermal current, helped concentrate these nucleotides inside the vent, which builds up and forms ribonucleic acid (RNA). This process continues to produce more RNA. Recent research has proved that RNA acted as auto catalysts, replicating without the aid of enzymes like today.

Later on, iron-sulfur biofilms are encased in a phospholipid membrane containing self-replicable RNA and other important organic matter. Phospholipid membranes, with one water-soluble and one water-insoluble end, spontaneously aggregate into a bilayer, forming a stable barrier separating the cell's interior from its external environment. Thus, the first cell evolved. These primitive cells dissolved and evolved countless times as they circulated the vent. Once stabilized, these phospholipid membranes grew and divided, giving more cells a successful reproduction.

## THE FIRST BREATH

Thus, the cells are formed with a phospholipid membrane encasing self-replicating RNA within, but the question is how these cells thrived, powered up, or breathed life into it. The secret lies in the chemical composition and resulting pH difference between the alkaline vent and the acidic seawater, which helped produce the required energy through an electrochemical gradient.

The diffusion of ions from higher to lower gradients and the difference between acidic seawater and alkaline vents produced an electrical potential, generating energy that fueled our primordial cells.

The pyrophosphate allowed the cells to extract more energy from the gradient difference between the seawater and the vent. In due course, ATP synthase evolved and started producing the energy ATP. These reactions mirrored present-day glycolysis, the anaerobic breakdown of glucose to lactic acid, yielding a net energy gain of two molecules of ATP.

# THE FIRST VOYAGE

Some cells located farther from the main vent, where the natural electrochemical gradient was weaker, began generating their own gradients by pumping protons across their membranes. They utilized the energy from the reaction between carbon dioxide and hydrogen to do so. This reaction released only a small amount of energy, not enough to produce sufficient ATP directly. The cells repeatedly performed the reaction, gradually storing the energy as and when it was produced. Over time, this allowed them to accumulate sufficient energy to eventually produce ATP.

Thus, when the lipid cell membrane and the capabilities to produce and store the ATP were achieved, they were no longer tied to the vents. Cells left the vents on two different occasions, leading to bacteria and archaea. To navigate the water world, these ancient explorers developed simple yet effective flagella, a whip-like appendage that propelled them through the water. Endless variants of unicellular organisms are formed. They conquered the nook and corner of the whole earth, from hot sulfur vents and deep ocean to the freezing depth of Antarctic lakes. This was the first invasion of Earth.

## IMPLICATIONS:

- Our cells still maintain a carbon and hydrogen-rich environment like the first microbe of the earth.

- Our cells still encompass the medium of water and salt,

similar to the sea, which got entrapped when the first cell formed.

- In humans, RNA still does a lot of essential cellular work, like splitting genes, assembling proteins, etc., which may be the leftovers of the age before the DNA world.

- Iron-sulfur still acts as a catalyst in many reactions to our bodies. It may be the oldest enzyme.

- The phosphatase enzyme is still found in many bacteria and archaea.

- All present-day cells carry out glycolysis, indicating that these reactions arose early in evolution.

# CHAPTER 2

## GASSES

*"Man was created of the earth, and lives by virtue of the air; for there is in the air a secret food of life... whose invisible congealed spirit is better than the whole earth."* - Michael Sendivogius.

### CARBON DIOXIDE

When life originated about 4.3 billion years ago, the Earth was not as we see it today. It was like an alien world shown in some high-budget Hollywood movies. Earth was naked; devoid of any ocean and atmosphere, nothing existed. Asteroids, like huge nuclear bombs, had wreaked havoc everywhere. The atmosphere was dense with Hydrogen and Helium when it originated. But these chemicals are very light in weight and quickly escape into space. Earth was recovering from a war zone-like scenario.

Even worse was the moon-forming impact around 4.5 billion years ago, shortly after the creation of Earth. A massive body in the solar system smashed into Earth, throwing molten material into space that merged to form the moon. This blow created a meltdown of the earth's crust, creating an everlasting scar on the face of Mother Earth. As an ill-effect, she spitted her golden red blood, magma, all over the place. But these volcanic eruptions gave us a second atmosphere, a chance for our emergence, where even hydrogen and helium shied to stay. This blow dispersed vast quantities of water steam, carbon dioxide, nitrous oxide, ammonia, and methane, making our sky murky and reddish-brown.

As our earth cooled, the water vapor in the atmosphere started to condense and rain out over the barren earth, forming our mighty ocean. Like an epic love story, the rain brought carbon dioxide to the sea, a highly soluble gas in the water.

The carbon dioxide concentration increased in the ancient ocean, dropping the seawater pH towards 5-7, and it also acted as a precursor for forming organic molecules in due course. The pH in the alkaline hydrothermal vents was about 10-11. This easily created a significant pH difference of 5-6 units between the ocean and the alkaline hydrothermal vents. When these fluids flowed across the thin semiconducting iron-sulfur biofilm, the difference in the pH helped reduce carbon dioxide with hydrogen-producing organic molecules like carbon monoxide, formate, and formaldehyde.

Carbon dioxide may be a villain today. We produce it and discard it as waste material through our little nostrils. Environmentalists scream about rising greenhouse gases and resulting global warming. It is a tremendous headache to think, and let us come to it later.

However, the situation was different in the Hadean eon. Carbon dioxide from the earth's womb flew to the limitless sky and then back, creating a soupy ocean where the magic of creation unfolded. Carbon dioxide became the backbone of life, nurturing it with care. This silent architect hummed the song of life on the earth.

## IMPLICATION

- Carbon dioxide not only helped the first cell to originate but continues to provide us with energy via photosynthesis, a very close relationship.

- Carbon dioxide concentrations in the blood help maintain the pH level for smooth functioning, and changes in the brain trigger chemoreceptors and help regulate respiration.

## NITROGEN

*"The nitrogen in our DNA, the calcium in our teeth, the iron in our blood, the carbon in our apple pies were made in the interiors of collapsing stars. **WE ARE MADE OF STARSTUFF.**" - Carl Sagan*

Volcanic eruptions and lightning discharges in the Hadean and Archaean eons produced nitric oxide from carbon dioxide and nitrogen. Pouring rain brought nitrogen to Earth in the form of nitric oxide, nitrate, and nitrogen dioxide.

## HEMOGLOBIN

But as it is now, nitrogen was toxic then, too. Our marvelous ancestors came up with a solution, and it is hemoglobin's. To be precise, it is an early form of hemoglobin called Nitric oxide binding heam's. Our microbial ancestors invented hemoglobin's not as a vehicle to carry oxygen but to bind the nitric oxide and to detoxify it. But they didn't stop there. Every disaster was an opportunity for them. They convert nitric oxide into inert nitrate, which is then used to synthesize amino acids, the building block of life. Marvelous, isn't it?

In an oxygen-depleted atmosphere, nitric oxide acts as a high-energy oxidant. It is also a suitable electron acceptor and helps redox reactions in autotrophic metabolism, a process by which a living thing can make its own food from simple chemical substances, such as carbon dioxide or carbonates and an inorganic nitrogen compound, especially in alkaline hydrothermal vents.

## BORING BILLION

Although the earth was a disaster for us to be in the Hadean and Archean eons, the mid-Proterozoic eon between 1.8 to 0.8 billion years was less dramatic. Even geologists term it a boring billion, but the latest finding shows it had some interesting turns.

Jeniffer Glass, a biogeochemist at the Georgia Institute of Technology in Atlanta, suggests that during the mid-Proterozoic, the ferrous ion in seawater reacted rapidly with nitrogen molecules, especially nitric oxide, yielding nitrous oxide in a process called chemo denitrification. These nitrous oxides bubbled up into the atmosphere. Her experiments suggested that the nitrous oxide levels in Proterozoic eons were significantly higher, about ten times greater than today's level of 0.00003%. Eventually, early microbes breathed laughing gas just as many microbes do today. The enzymes these microbes used to breathe nitric and nitrous oxide combine to create cytochrome C oxidase, which helps us breathe oxygen.

These significant evolutionary changes occurred amid the Young Sun paradox, a term first coined by the astronomer Carl Sagan in 1972, referring to how the sun was about 10% less luminous than it is today. Under such low-light conditions, Earth should have been frozen, but it wasn't, thanks to the greenhouse gases that kept the Earth habitable. Gasses like nitrous oxide, carbon dioxide, and methane kept the earth warmer by about 37 to 41 degrees Fahrenheit, an increased heat that prevented the world from a global ice age.

## AS A DEFENSE PERSONAL

In its infancy, when life was learning to breathe nitrogen, it faced another challenge: the rising atmospheric oxygen level. We will deep-dive into this in the next section. One of the implications of rising oxygen was the formation of ozone. Sunlight breaks oxygen molecules and rearranges them with additional oxygen, producing ozone, a threat to the fragile cells of primitive microorganisms.

To avoid this unwelcome guest, ozone, organisms produce nitric oxide and eliminate it in their surroundings, creating a shield around them. Then, these nitric oxides bind with the ozone, neutralizing the toxic gas and preventing it from causing damage to the cell wall. This little success against the ozone encouraged the organisms to implement these strategies inside the cells to control oxygen toxicity.

Nitrogen offered a lifeline, providing organisms the stability they need to thrive without oxygen. First, life invented hemoglobin to nullify the toxicity of nitric oxide. Then, these organisms learned to turn inert nitrogen gas into ammonia, which are the building blocks for amino acids, and intelligently incorporated them into the biological systems. They are used as defense mechanisms by our primitive microbes when life faces the problem of rising atmospheric oxygen. Later, the enzymes utilized to breathe laughing gas were recruited for breathing oxygen. Thus, nitrogen helped bridge the gap between the ancient, oxygen-free Earth and the present, oxygen-rich world.

Oxygen is a vital gas for today's organisms, but that was not true then because the primordial earth lacked oxygen. Organisms learn to breathe and eliminate other gasses before daring to try oxygen. There were a lot more severe experiments and sacrifices made for the sake of existence. Even in this oxygenated earth, where oxygen is the dominant force in respiration, nitrogen never loses its importance. The nitrogen cycle, established by those early organisms, became mandatory, without which the modern earth could not flourish.

## IMPLICATION

- Nitric oxide was developed into a transmitter for inter- and intra-cellular signaling. It can freely cross the cell membrane without the help of a receptor, which means that it acted as a transmitter before the evolution of cellular receptors.

- Still, ozone is used as a powerful disinfectant against microorganisms.

- Nitric oxide is produced in human bodies to reduce free radical damage.

- Nasal nitric oxide levels are found to be increased by 15 to 20 fold during humming.

- Nitric oxide, carbon monoxide, and hydrogen sulfide are abundant elements in primitive Earth and are linked with evolution. Our system still effectively utilizes them as signaling molecules, regulating oxygen delivery.

- Nitric oxide is critical for mitochondrial functioning. A deficiency leads to fatigue due to mitochondrial dysfunction. Beetroots are the best source of inorganic nitrates.

- Nitric oxide increases the vasodilation of the blood vessels, thereby increasing blood flow and proportionately increasing the oxygen supply to the tissues.

- RBCs are regulators of three gas respiratory cycles that supply oxygen to the tissue and the removal of carbon dioxide from tissues. They also use nitric oxide for vasodilation and help in more oxygen delivery to tissues.

## OXYGEN

*"He gave life to the breath- oxygen, a simple gas, he transferred into words, ideas, hope." - Michael J. Fox*

The world's biggest pollution crisis was witnessed 2 billion years ago during the Proterozoic eon from 2.4 billion to 1.8 billion years, almost 80 - 99.5% of organisms, then microbes were killed mercilessly in the world's cruelest massacre. The villain in the story is our hero, Oxygen, our vital gas. It is a story where the hero, the originator of life, becomes the villain discarded mercilessly, and the villain becomes the superhero, the savior of life.

## A NEW DAWN

With mutation and replication, microbes thrived. They left their beloved home, alkaline hydrothermal vents, and started exploring the vast earth with great amusement. The need for carbon and hydrogen was always daunting. Hydrothermal vent fluids were an excellent supply of hydrogen. Once abundant, carbon dioxide in the primordial ocean started depleting as the population increased massively. For an analogy, the atoms in space comprise 91% hydrogen. The atmosphere of Mars and Venus still has about 95% carbon dioxide, whereas it is 0.03% on Earth. The starved microbes searching for hydrogen realized the unlimited source surrounding them: water. However, the loving relationship between hydrogen and oxygen molecules in water was challenging to break. Water is a highly stable molecule.

Around 2.7 billion years ago, ancestors of cyanobacteria who were well-trained to utilize hydrogen sulfide to convert carbon dioxide into organic molecules- a pathway of photosynthesis still used by some bacteria were fine-tuned to tackle the new challenge. They solved the problem by using sunlight as a lethal weapon to break the relationship between hydrogen and oxygen. Higher energy light at short wavelengths is used to split the hydrogen from the water. The hydrogen combined with the carbon dioxide produced organic molecules such as sugars; thus, cyanobacteria thrived. This little invention changed the future of Earth's history into a more scenic and greener one.

## OXYGEN HOLOCAUST

Stories always have twists; Cyano used the hydrogen, but what about the oxygen left out? Excess oxygen reacted with the minerals, metals, and gasses available in the atmosphere, rocks, and the ocean for millions of years. Almost every chemical was oxidized. About 4500 minerals are present on the earth today, and 2500 are produced during this great oxidation event. Most oxygen is in solid forms, such as oxides and silicates, not gas. The total amount of oxygen in the atmosphere, oceans, and living creatures is less than 0.05% compared to the total mass of oxygen in the whole Earth. Thus, the once-reduced earth got oxidized.

With an almost inexhaustible hydrogen source, the cyanobacteria were very successful. They spread over the earth's surface and reached the nook and corner; their only requirement was water and light, and they increased like anything. This successful expansion created more trouble as oxygen accumulated. About 2.4 billion years ago, oxygen started bubbling up into the atmosphere from 0.0001% and surged to 10% by the end of the great oxidation event. The whole earth has become a toxic gas chamber in which life suffocated to survive. Sunlight and oxygen separately are lethal bombs to organisms, but when they are both hands together, they are like powerful nuclear missiles.

Oxygen grabbed electrons and produced free radicals, which were short-lived and highly reactive and caused severe damage to the cells. Oxygen is like a playboy; it combines with carbon, hydrogen, sulfur, nitrogen, nucleic acid, amino acids, lipids, vitamins, etc. The first victims were cyanobacteria itself and the non-mobile microbes. The mounting oxygen level in the biosphere left the microbes with no alternative but to protect themselves from molecular oxygen or face the death sentence. Bio luminous, synthesis of vitamin E and oxygen binding of hemoglobins are some of the defense mechanisms invented by microbes for their survival.

Oxygen tolerance was improved with further mutation and transfer of successful DNA patterns among the surviving bacterial species. These new resistant bacteria quickly multiplied and replaced most of the oxygen-sensitive bacteria. Others hide beneath the oxygen-resistant bacterial mat and oxygen-deprived areas like mud and soil.

## A TALE OF SURVIVAL

Ultimately, cyanobacteria devised a plan to utilize the same oxygen for its energy needs with a new metabolic pathway. Thus, aerobic respiration started and developed oxidative metabolism. Oxygen is a highly reactive molecule. This new metabolic pathway utilized this reactivity and generated more energy from organic molecules, producing carbon dioxide and water as waste material. This is the story of how the hero and villain got swapped.

Aerobic metabolism was far more effective than anaerobic glycolysis. Earlier, the microbes could only produce 2 ATP, but now, with the help of oxygen, they can produce 36-38 ATP. The small size of oxygen gives high intracellular diffusivity, and the correct redox potential is utilized as an electron acceptor in energy production. This extra energy spearheaded the evolution.

Cyanobacteria is now a self-sufficient organism with some precursors; it can form whatever is required to survive, like nucleic acid, protein vitamins, etc. It evolved into hundreds of different types and formed the bottom of the food chain. With self-sufficiency, it conquered the whole world.

Other types of bacteria depended on the cyanobacteria for food needs and slowly adapted to aerobic respiration. Microbes maintain the oxygen balance of the atmosphere by producing oxygen;

some consume the same, maintaining the balance of this highly toxic gas.

As atmospheric oxygen increased, ozone formed and built up in the stratosphere. Ozone helped absorb lethal solar radiation from reaching the earth's surface, paving the way for terrestrial evolution.

For life to breathe oxygen, was like walking on a delicate thread. Oxygen is a vital gas, but unfortunately, it is also a lethal toxin. The story of oxygen shows the power of evolution, which empowered living beings to extract the enormous power they held while mitigating their potential threat. However, life on Earth successfully learned to breathe oxygen.

## IMPLICATION

- After the oxygen rise, nitric oxide and carbon monoxide became less attractive to electron acceptors, and hydrogen sulfide was eliminated as an electron donor. However, these chemicals are still used in many physiological functions and as gasotransmitters.

- It is estimated that around 2-3% of the oxygen taken up by aerobic cells produces oxygen free radicals and hydrogen peroxide.

- Nuclear membranes are formed around the nucleus to control oxygen toxicity and minimize free radical attacks. Thus, the nucleus provides an anoxic and safe environment for protecting DNA.

# CHAPTER 3

SYMBIOSIS

*"You are not an encapsulated bag of skin dragging around a dreary little ego. You are an evolution-ary wonder, a trillion cells singing together in a vast chorale, an organism-environment, a symbiosis of cell and soul."* - Jean Houston.

Aerobic eukaryotes emerged within a few hundred million years after the great oxidation event about 2.3 billion years ago. Their birth story is like a love story and is of particular interest due to the presence of mitochondria, the powerhouse of cells without which breathing cannot be completed. More than 20 different versions of endosymbiotic theory explain the origin of eukaryotes and their mitochondria. The most relatable hypothesis is the hydrogen hypothesis, published in 1988 by William Martin and Miklos Muller.

It is a story of breakup and pickup. A small recap: When the early prokaryotes achieved energy-self-sufficiency and protective lipid membranes, they left the alkaline hydrothermal vents billions of years ago on two different occasions, leading to two different lineages: bacteria and archaea.

## A LOVE STORY

Going in, the reunion tale of two distinct prokaryotic organisms continues. The archaea hate oxygen; they are primarily anaerobes and require hydrogen to produce ATP for survival. In an anoxic environment, an archaeon was attracted to a bacteria capable of producing energy without the help of oxygen, which produces hydrogen as a byproduct. This story happened in the interior of stromatolite, a mat-like sedimentary structure formed by colonies of microorganisms compressed into a stone-like structure. The archaeon's dependency on hydrogen created an intense selective pressure for the two organisms to remain nearby. Over time, this led to intimate interactions between the two cells, driving the unification of the two organisms into a more complex primitive eukaryotic cell. This process is known as endosymbiosis, where one organism lives inside another.

The bacteria were capable of both anaerobic metabolism and aerobic respiration. Its ability to switch between anaerobic hydrogen production and aerobic respiration allowed the new couple to thrive in varying environmental conditions. With mutual gene transfers, metabolic pathways are integrated. Gradually, the bacterium's respiratory capabilities contributed to developing mitochondria, which helped produce ATP.

As an English science-fiction writer, John Wyndham said, *"The distance - and the difference - between us dwindled and vanished. We could meet, mingle, and blend. Neither one of us existed anymore; for a time, there was a single being that was both. There was escape from the solitary cell, a brief symbiosis, sharing all the words."*

Their relationship was so loving that neither could live without the other. The new eukaryote entirely depended on the bacterial cell to meet its energy requirements. Whereas bacterial cells lost most of their DNA and the ability to produce proteins, they became highly productive and efficient at producing ATP. When energy requirements increase, more mitochondria are cloned, giving enormous energy, which paves the way for the evolution of complex life.

The eukaryotes developed cilia, making them possible for a romantic getaway. In single-cell organisms like Paramecia, cilia cover their entire surface, beating rhythmically to propel them through their aquatic environment.

## A STRONG FOUNDATION

The exact time of the origin of life and eukaryote evolution is an ongoing debate. At least eukaryotes developed 2.3 billion years ago, leaving a space of approximately 2 billion years of prokaryotic evolution. For the first two billion years, life on Earth was inhabited solely by bacteria. Before complex organisms are born, most biochemical metabolic pathways are finely tuned. They developed flawless blueprints for fermentation, photosynthesis, metabolic pathways, cellular respiration, nitrification, denitrification, etc. They are the first genetic engineers capable of transferring bits of genetic material for the successful propagation of other species.

Aerobic metabolism granted an efficient process of energy production that was important for building, servicing, and maintaining the infrastructural integrity of complex cells and tissues. The advantage of aerobic metabolism is that it produces 18 times more free metabolic energy when compared to anaerobic pathways. With this surplus energy, the air was primed to support the evolution of complex animal and plant life. Subsequently, oxygen became an indispensable factor in the aerobic metabolism of higher animals. The formation of the ozone layer paved the way for the terrestrial invasion of life. They transformed the earth's surface and atmosphere, preparing us to live sophisticatedly.

The evolution of prokaryotes and eukaryotes was slow and gradual, laying the groundwork for our evolution. Then, about 600 million years ago, Earth experienced a rapid evolution, driven by the availability of energetic oxygen and the biochemical solid foundation established by our bacterial ancestors.

The sacrifices, starvation, and suffocation that our microbial ancestors went through are unimaginable. The innovations, discoveries, alliances, and mutual support at tough times are astonishing. Life multiplied and occupied every nook and corner of this world, not by killing or waging war on each other, but by co-opting and networking. Evolution is not just an account of our past, but also an account of morals and values to learn and live by. Humans have a lot to learn and imbibe from our single-celled ancestors.

## IMPLICATION

- Mitochondria in humans share several bacterial characteristics, such as their ability to multiply and synthesize proteins and sensitivity to antibiotics. Overusing antibiotics harms infectious bacteria and can also affect mitochondria, which possess these bacterial-like properties.

- Chloroplast is also a product of endosymbiosis, a love saga between photosynthetic cyanobacteria and an eukaryotic cell.

- Like prokaryotic bacteria, mitochondria and chloroplasts have their genetic code, undergo binary fusion, and are the same size and shape.

## MULTICELLULAR ORGANISM

*"Life on Earth is such a good story you cannot afford to miss the beginning... Beneath our superficial differences, we are all of us walking communities of bacteria. The world shimmers, a pointillist landscape made of tiny living beings."* -Lynn Margulis

Throughout evolution, microbes did not pause; they kept on socializing and inventing. Their collaboration and alliance led to a new form of life: multicellularity. Fossil evidence of 1.6 billion-year-old red algae suggests multicellularity must have evolved much earlier.

Some unicellular eukaryotes joined to form multicellular aggregates, eventually evolving into multicellular organisms. Multicellularity occurs in two ways. In cells without a cell wall, special proteins called cell adhesion molecules act like glue, holding the cells together. Cells with a wall modify the wall biogenesis to inhibit the final split, separating them into individual cells. As a result, the daughter cells remain fused. Interestingly, preventing this final split is often easier to achieve.

Unicells tend to achieve multicellularity, but organizing them into tissues and organs was tough. The genetic material of the cells contains DNA sequences with information to make thousands of different proteins and RNA molecules. The genome in every cell is typically the same. The cells are different not due to the distinct genetic information they possess, but because a cell generally expresses only a fraction of its genes. Different types of cells in multicellular organisms arise because different sets of genes are expressed. The pattern of genes they express changes in response to environmental changes such as the signals from other cells. The most important task of controlling gene expression lies with our old hero RNA.

Around 470 million years ago, the green algae Volvox carteri cells, which are eukaryotes, aggregate with each other and form multicellular colonies, considered the evolutionary precursor of present-day plants, which made our earth a beautiful place to live in, drastically changing the planet's ecology.

The last common ancestor of animals evolved from a single-cell ancestor more than 600 million years ago. As they are soft-bodied, we have no fossil evidence of their appearance. They were small and tended to stay still or creep slowly across the ocean bed. The idea behind maintaining complex organisms lies with careful and craftful cell specialization, high coordination, and division of labor among the cells. Otherwise, it would be a mess.

Like our unicellular ancestors, life in the time of multicellular origin was also dramatic. The Ediacaran period, which spanned 635 - 541 million years, was part of an era of extreme tectonic, geochemical, and evolutionary changes that changed marine ecosystems. The supercontinent Rodinia began to break up, leading to volcanic activities. Sometimes, the bad things that happen lead to the best things that can ever happen. These tectonic outbursts introduced large quantities of nutrients into the oceans. The seafloors were covered by communities of microbes, which formed mm to cm-thick microbial mats. This nutrition-rich seabed provided the nourishment and stability for larger organisms. Like a cherry on the cake, the earth's ocean became fully oxygenated. Oxygen began penetrating deeper oceans and building up in the water and atmosphere. Before this period, the deep sea was considered anoxic, apart from shallow water.

Against this backdrop of climatic, tectonic, and geochemical conditions, the organisms transformed from simple structured microbial mats to more complex organisms and radiated around the globe. Some had typical bodies, heads, tails, etc. Primitive organisms don't need a stomach, intestines, or lungs. Simple nutrients and oxygen slip in and out of their cell walls through diffusion.

These organisms have a high body surface area-to-volume ratio to facilitate osmosis.

Unicellular organisms are far more abundant than multicellular organisms and have been around for an additional 2 billion years, with the potential to outlive them in the future. This raises a fascinating question: why did some lineages evolve to become multicellular? If unicellularity was such a huge success, what's unique in achieving multicellularity? One reason is that multicellularity increases body size, helping organisms escape predators. Additionally, resource bartering allows different cell types to specialize in producing essential resources, giving the whole system access to more nutrients. Multicellularity also offers stress protection, where outer cells shield inner cells from harsh chemicals and physical stress, enhancing the organism's survival. Finally, the division of labor among cells enables specialization in various tasks, improving the organism's ability to navigate and gather nutrients effectively.

Achieving multicellularity was easy. Unicells had this basic instinct to aggregate themselves to form colonies or microbial mats. They were just waiting for the right time and situation. Once they got it, they achieved it with ease. The origin of multicellularity represents a leap from simplicity to complexity with the power of cooperation and innovation. This transformation laid the foundation for the incredible diversity of life, from simple algae to complex animals and plants.

## IMPLICATION

- Almost all multi-cellular organisms retain their unicellular phases like eggs, sperm, zygote, etc.

- Animals evolved in close association with many bacteria and eukaryotes, and this association with microbiota developed animal gut biota.

- The ratio of human cells to that of microorganisms in the human body is closer to a 1:1 ratio.

- A disadvantage of being multicellular is the formation of cancerous cells on aging.

- David Goode, a computational cancer biologist at Peter MacCallum Cancer Center in Melbourne, Australia, and colleagues examined gene expression in seven types of solid tumors. They found that the genes dated back to early single-celled eukaryotic organisms are activated in causing cancer. In multicellularity, the genes are evolved to stop cell division at an appropriate time. However, the genes suited to a unicellular lifestyle drive the growth of the tumor, forgetting to stop the cell division.

- Some scientists even argue that plants have cancerous cells.

# CHAPTER 4

# AQUATIC BREATHING



*"Water is life's matter and matrix, mother and medium. There is no life without water."* -Albert Szent-Gyorgyi

Everything was designed with supreme care and fine-tuned to perfection in the vast microbial world through ages of experimentation. It was complex then, but now, for our eyes, it seems simple. Breath was not an exception, either.

## SIMPLE BREATHING

The tiny single-celled organisms floating happily in the mighty ocean learned to breathe by applying the basic physics of diffusion and used partial pressure gradient for its advantage. This little creature, separated from the environment by a delicate, almost invisible membrane, generously traded carbon dioxide for vibrant oxygen. They were in no hurry; they knew diffusion was a slow, passive process. Diffusion-based gas exchange is best suited for tiny multicellular organisms that are highly flattened, like flatworms, where nearly every cell touches the external environment, ensuring a steady supply of oxygen to all the cells. This diffusion is the key to survival for primitive organisms like sponges and comb jellies. However, there are some limitations. If the cells are large and thick, diffusion will nourish only the outermost cells exposed or the cells that are close to the environment. It cannot provide oxygen to the innermost cells.

Evolution is a process without any specific purpose or direction. It unfolds according to the ongoing environmental happenings. It can't be controlled or have a predetermined path to travel. Variations in genes arise spontaneously, shaped by the needs and pressures the organisms face. It is also important to remember that evolution has not only given success stories; many times, organisms have also faced extinction. Evolution is a natural experiment set up in the vast lab named Earth, constantly testing and reshaping life without any specific goal.

## AN EXPLOSION

Although life originated in anoxic conditions, evolution was propelled by oxygen. When living organisms are exposed to oxygen, the surge of energy they receive keeps them from evolving into more advanced organisms. Increased availability of oxygen in seawater during the Cambrian period 541 -485 million years ago created an explosion in the ocean; this time, it was not the volcanoes but living beings. Complex life quickly emerged and diversified. This is known as the Cambrian explosion, which created a complex, watery world of animal species.

Unicells and small multicellular organisms are self-sufficient, drawing the nutrients and energy they need directly from their environment; they can take care of themselves. However, as the organisms grew, the energy and resources had to be shared among them, creating new problems like delivering oxygen to the tissues, clearing waste, etc.

They are not militants. They are peace lovers. They know the more they share, the more they will have. To overcome this problem, they started to organize, leading to the morphological differentiation of groups of cells and arranging them to become tissue and organs, and later on to developed systems like the respiratory, cardiovascular, digestive, etc. This is achieved by selective gene expression. With each new adaptation, the size of organisms that could be sustained increased. They grew more diverse, branching into countless forms, resulting in the immense diversity of multicellular organisms.

## INNER JELLY

Bacterial infestation is not only a challenge for us today, but it was so millions of years ago. The primitive creatures, like the body of sponges, are lined with bacteria. Later on, as anemones, corals, jellyfish, comb jellies, etc, evolved a barrier across their body. They just smeared them with a layer of anti-bacterial slime named mucus. They secreted mucus in large quantities whenever required. This is the first line of defense for many organisms, including us. Mucus acts as an antibacterial barrier and is used for feeding and cleaning surfaces from dust and debris. Mucin, a protein found in mucus, has binding sites that mimic the cell surface, tricking bacteria into binding to it. Unaware they've been cheated, the bacteria stick to the mucus, thus preventing them from reaching and infecting the cells.

The once peaceful and calm waters started to change. Slowly, bloody wars erupted. This complex world created competition among fellow beings. There was a push-and-pull race between the prey and predators. Every organism evolved to escape predation and sharpen its tools to become good predators. Survival was a key to evolution.

Among them, the small and simple fishlike creature Cephy, a cephalochordate, was mastering the art of filter feeding, which later in the chapter on evolutionary history had a profound impact. Their earliest fossil records date back to 525 million years in the early Cambrian period.

We know gill slits are individual openings to gills and are used by organisms for respiration in water. Cephy had one, but the purpose was not respiration; it was designed for feeding. They loved feeding planktonic microorganisms. They drew water into the mouth, and the surrounding tentacles formed a grid that kept sand and other larger particles out of the mouth. This water passes through the narrow perforations known as pharyngeal gill slits. They extend two-thirds of the animal's length, starting from the mouth. As the water passes through these slits, the larger particles suspended in the water get entrapped in a layer of mucus that moves upward along the gill slits. Then, the nutrition-rich mucus is rolled up and transported to the intestine, where food is digested and absorbed. The success of particle feeding depends upon the ability of mucus to be dragged as a connected sheet or string with the help of cilia. For breathing, Cephy still depends on the skin.

The water that flowed through the gill slits for filter feeding was later co-opted for breathing and facilitated the evolution of larger and more active fishes following a predatory lifestyle. This change of gill slits from feeding to respiration replaced the skin as the primary breathing site, and the evolution of gills was undertaken. Cephy's story is a testament to the incredible power of evolution. It shows how traits are developed and adapted to new functions, ensuring species' survival. The simplest creature like Cephy adjusted and thrived through challenges that forever shaped the course of life on earth. Organisms without spines lay the groundwork for the evolution of respiratory organs.

## IMPLICATION

- The pharyngeal apparatus serves the dual function of respiration and feeding in many species.

- Pharyngeal arches develop during embryogenesis and give rise to many of the neurovascular and musculoskeletal systems in the head and neck. The complexity of the pharyngeal apparatus's development can lead to birth defects.

- Studies on the early evolution of mucus isolated from several species of jellyfish revealed that it possessed a qniumucin gene, which showed a surprising structural similarity to MUC5AC, an important mucin found in the human stomach and lungs.

- Mucus helps clean bacteria, dust, and debris from the lungs. It is produced in humans' eyes, mouth, nose, sinuses, lungs, throat, stomach, intestine, and reproductive organs.

## MORPHOLOGICAL FEATURES OF GAS EXCHANGERS

*"The organs are the horses, the mind is the rein, the intellect is the charioteer, the soul is the rider, and the body is the chariot. The master of the household, the King, the Self of man, is sitting in this chariot."*
—— Swami Vivekananda

As complex organisms originated, the system that supported them also grew complex. Every system has basic principles to follow to achieve its purpose and to do its duty flawlessly. Still, at this point in evolution, the skin acted as a suitable gas exchanger; it effectively took oxygen and expelled carbon dioxide through diffusion. However, as organisms grow in size, they must masterly craft organs for the specific purpose of gas exchangers so that oxygen can enter deep inside the organisms and nourish every cell with this vital energy.

It is a chicken and egg paradox where complex and energetic organisms evolved due to the evolution of efficient respiratory organs or vice versa. Factors that influenced the evolution of breathing apparatus are behavior, body size, and the environment of the species in which it lived. As the organism is more active, a steady oxygen supply is required to maintain its activity. As a result, highly active tiny organisms have relatively better-refined gas exchangers than inactive large organisms. Thus, the efficiency of the gas exchange mainly depends on activity, such as mobility, rather than size.

## A WELL THOUGHT OUT PLAN

The gas exchangers developed as an evagination, where structures extend outward like gills, or invagination, where they fold inward like lungs. These helped organisms achieve a large surface area, and further stratification and compartmentalization of these organs maximized the surface area within the limits of small spaces like multistoried buildings built in a sprawling metropolitan city. These large surface areas improve the contact points between the medium (liquid or gas) and that of the gas exchanger, thus optimizing the surface area and ensuring they absorb the maximum amount of oxygen and expel carbon dioxide effectively.

The membrane of the gas exchangers was thinly partitioned and kept moistened so that rapid diffusion of respiratory gas can be achieved, which is critical for life. An extensive network of blood vessels was developed within the gas exchangers. This vascularisation resembles the complex network of highways and public transportation systems that crisscross the city. This network helps increase the exposure of blood volume to the respiratory medium. The blood vessels increase the transport of gasses between the respiratory surface and the body cells, which is crucial for maintaining energy and activity, just like the transportation network in a buzzing city.

The organ's geometric organization is something to be amazed at, like a strategically planned city grid, where every road, infrastructure, and pace is meticulously planned. The spatial arrangement of the respiratory systems was accurately planned. Every fold, chamber, and vessel was placed to ensure optimal interaction with the surrounding air or water. This organization enhanced the respiratory system's efficiency, ensuring every breath counted.

The structure of gas exchange is a well-thought-out plan that has evolved in remarkable ways across different species, optimizing the balance between efficient oxygen uptake and carbon dioxide elimination. These adaptations, whether seen in the structure of gills, lungs, or even at the cellular level, highlight the delicate relationship between form and function in sustaining life.

## FISH

*"Every innovation, every invention used by tetrapods on land, originally appeared in some form in fish, including lungs, appendages, and now feeding."* -Neil Shubin.

Life on Earth during the Cambrian period dramatically differed from today; the animals looked bizarre and had unusual body planes. We would be scared to death if we were ill-fated to be there. Rising sea levels and high tectonic activities contributed to changes in seawater chemistry through hydrothermal processes that released rich sources of minerals and altered the composition of the Cambrian Ocean. The oxygen solubility increased, and the ocean was brimming with life-essential chemicals like calcium, magnesium, sulfate, phosphate, etc.

Due to this sudden increase in calcium concentrations during the early Cambrian era, organisms began to precipitate calcium carbonate and calcium phosphate to manage and detoxify the excess calcium in the environment. Thus, bio mineralization helped organisms regulate internal chemistry and protected them against environmental stressors. Moreover, with its new fancy armor, it was a gala party with life-essential nutrients and energetic oxygen.

## AGE-OLD GILL

Around 530 million years ago, early chordates developed the skull and spine, leading to the origin of vertebrates. From there, jawless fishes started to evolve. Haggy, a hagfish, is a very ancient and evolutionarily significant group; they are eel-shaped, jawless fish with no bone, have a single tail and rudimentary vertebrae, and they had gills. The catch is that the gills are not the primary gas exchangers; 80- 90% of oxygen uptake in hagfishes occurs across the skin at rest.

Haggy feasts happily on dead animals, using its toothed tongue to enter dead animal carcasses. While feeding, it takes extended periods, which lead to low oxygen and an elevated carbon dioxide concentration. This severely affects the acid-base balance of Haggy's fragile body. Without proper mechanisms in place, elevated pH will disrupt protein and enzyme function, affecting cellular ion transportation, muscle contractility, and metabolism. Haggy's gill is an effective structure for maintaining the acid-base balance.

The Ediacaran and the early Cambrian periods witnessed minor to significant pH fluctuations due to the tectonic activities and the resulting inflow of minerals. As the size of organisms started to increase, it became hard for the skin to maintain pH levels alone. A necessity arose to build an effective system to monitor and maintain the pH balance; the primary selective pressure for vertebrate gills was maintaining the acid-base regulation. This helped the primitive species to roam the sea of varying salinity.

## A ROLE CHANGE

To survive the arms race on the seabed, vertebrates developed teeth, claws, and fins. Fins gave them extra power to their newly evolved teeth and jaws. The world's first predators took form and caused havoc in the sea with these extra fittings. This transition from a passive lifestyle to an active swimmer necessitated more oxygen. The gills started to take the lead and co-opted a central role in gas exchange.

The origin of the gill is a controversial topic. The ecto-endo-branchiate hypothesis is a scientific theory that proposes the gills of jawless vertebrates, such as lampreys and hagfish, and jawed vertebrates, including cartilaginous and bony fishes, evolved independently due to their distinct embryonic origins. This hypothesis was based on the observation that gills in jawless and jawed vertebrates originate from different regions of the embryonic epithelia. The gills of jawless vertebrates are derived from the endoderm, the innermost layer of cells in a developing embryo. Meanwhile, the gills of jawed vertebrates were developed from the ectoderm, the outermost layer of cells in the embryo. The theory suggests that because of these distinct developmental pathways, the gills in these two groups must have evolved independently from a common, gill-less ancestor. As a result, since the mid-20th century, the origin of gills has been thought of as a result of convergent evolution, where nature finds the same solution twice.

Dr. J. Andrew Gillis and Olivia R.A. Tidswell, University of Cambridge,'s research focuses on a humble creature: the little skate ( *Leucoraja erinacea*), a cartilaginous fish whose gills held secrets of the past. Stakes are an early branching lineage of jawed vertebrates, making them an excellent comparison point for inferring the anatomical development of the last common ancestor of jawed and jawless vertebrates.

They injected dye into the pharyngeal cavities of the stake embryos, and the dye spread, marking its way as they grew in the endodermal cells. Their findings were revolutionary; contrary to the long-held belief that jawed vertebrate gills derived from ectoderm, their skate embryos originated from the endoderm. This discovery suggests that the gills of both jawless and jawed vertebrates shared a common endodermal origin, pointing to a single evolutionary origin of pharyngeal gills before these two ancient lineages diverged. It shows gills originated deeper in evolutionary history than previously thought.

## A SUM UP

The exciting feature of pharyngeal gill slits in the primitive chordate was vital for their survival. They served as a sieve for trapping the food particles as water flowed through them; later, with the vascularization of these slits, the gas exchange occurred to some extent.

As time passed, some chordates ventured into a new evolutionary path, becoming jawless vertebrates like lampreys and hagfish. These creatures began to show a remarkable transformation. Water entered their mouths, passed through the pharyngeal slits, and reached the gill pouches within their bodies. There, the water bathed the gills and started using them as pH maintainers supported by gill arches that provided the structural foundation for more efficient water flow and greater surface area for gas exchange.

Around 400 million years ago, when jawed fish evolved, pharyngeal gill slits transformed. They thickened and grew more robust, eventually forming the earliest versions of jaws. With the development of jaws, the need for so many pharyngeal gill slits diminished. The once numerous slits began to reduce in number. The front most slits gradually became part of the jaws themselves. With time, gills became specialized organs of respiration, capable of extracting oxygen from water with remarkable efficiency.

The counter-current flow of water improves the efficiency of gills. That is, water enters through the fish's mouth and comes out through the gill slits in a direction that is opposite to the flow of blood in the gills. This provided a constant supply of oxygen to the body. Gills are well-planned structures in which 80-90% of dissolved oxygen is extracted from water. The efficiency is dramatically decreased to 10% if the direction of flow of one of the mediums is changed to the co-current system. Delicate gills are protected by the usual savior: the mucous membranes; they act as a physical and biochemical barrier against pathogens. Gills are superheroes performing multiple functions like eliminating $CO_2$ and ammonia, osmoregulation, acid-base balance, regulating circulatory hormones, and detoxifying harmful plasma-born substances.

Although the gills are rarely preserved due to their soft tissues, we have found a 525 million-year-old fossil of Haikouella lanceolata showing a clear presence of gill rays similar to that of modern fishes. This journey from primitive filter-feeding slits to highly specialized respiratory organs is etched in the fossil record and mirrored in the embryonic development of modern fish.

Fish with streamlined bodies and sophisticated gill structures glide through the water, drawing oxygen with each graceful movement. The gills, now complex and efficient, are proof of the evolutionary marvel that began with simple pharyngeal slits. It tells a story of adaptation, survival, and the relentless march of evolution, transforming simple structures into the sophisticated systems that sustain life in the oceans today.

## IMPLICATION:

- Gills are very delicate, almost paper-like structures that depend on the buoyancy of water to remain open.

- If the fish is taken out of the water, its fragile gills will stick together and collapse because air doesn't have the same density and buoyancy as water to keep the gills open and functioning. This is why a fish cannot live outside the water.

- Even if their gills did not collapse, they would eventually lose too much water from their bodies to survive as gills are outside the body.

- In the grand drama of evolution, fish gills evolved into humans' middle ear, allowing us to hear.

# PART-2

## PLEASANT LAND

# CHAPTER 5

# TERRESTRIAL BREATHING

*"Breathing is not only the process of inhaling and exhaling; it's a reminder that every breath we take is a gift of life."* –Unknown

Aquatic animals must learn to breathe air to leave the vast ocean and venture onto land. Breathing underwater was an art they mastered over millions of years of patient evolution. To breathe air, they again waited patiently for evolution to take its course. They need more than lungs. They need a detailed blueprint of mechanisms to regulate, control, and maintain the airflow and integrity of the structure.

## A GIFT FROM METAZOANS

This story dates long before the origin of lungs and even before vertebrates. It's a tale about Surfactant; its origin is ancient, and its presence is noted in the gas mantle of invertebrates like mollusks and pulmonate snails, tracing its lineage to the earliest ancestors of the metazoans- the first multicellular organisms. As a newcomer, it helped in simple tasks like supporting the immune systems of ancient creatures from the unseen dangers of their environment. Surfactants originate from the epithelial cells lining the pharynx. When the gut evolved from the pharynx, these surfactant-producing epithelial cells migrated with them, helping in controlling fluid-fluid interactions between liquids of different viscosities like serum, mucous, etc., and also guarded the gut against pathogens.

As evolution progressed, these epithelial cells traveled with the air-filled outpouchings from the gut to form lungs. They are complex molecules with 90% lipids and 10% proteins. The surfactant structure resembles a mutant tadpole, with each head sprouting two tails. Their heads love water, whereas their fatty tails hate them. Our lungs are lined with a thin film of water; whose surface tension creates a strong force pulling the alveoli to collapse inward. Pulmonary surfactants, with their dual nature hydrophilic head in and hydrophobic tail out, control the surface tension by forming a film at the air-liquid interface of the lungs like an anti-glue. They are always fair in helping; even the narrowest airways remain open for smooth airflow.

Surfactant lipids are particularly vital during the initial phase of inflating a collapsed lung, and lungs will take care of further inflation. Without surfactants, inflating the lungs would be a costly affair in terms of energy consumption. Even more, the lipid composition in surfactants has constantly evolved, mainly to suit temperature throughout the history of vertebrates. The alveolar stability, compliance of mammalian lungs, and innate immunity have been the ever-evolving functions of surfactants.

## RHYTHM OF BREATH

Like the glorification of heroes, the water-to-land transition is credited to the capacity to inhale oxygen. The much more critical issue is the elimination of carbon dioxide. Oxygen is scarce in the ocean compared to land. Oxygen is around 30 times more abundant in air at sea level at 15 degrees Celsius. Fishes overcome this deficiency by flushing large amounts of water over the gills. Carbon dioxide loves water more than oxygen does. It just gets readily dissolved into the water; with such a vast quantity of water, it is a cakewalk. But the situation takes a U-turn when it comes to air breathing. As oxygen is abundant, tetrapods can satisfy their air hunger with a small air volume. Unfortunately, carbon dioxide levels are equal in air and water. Thus, eliminating carbon dioxide was the real challenge in tetrapod evolution. Evolution, like Beethoven, took a peculiar behavior from one of our ancestors and repurposed it to compose a rhythm for our breath.

That universal beat was developed millions of years before the development of lungs. Lampreys, a jawless fish, do not have lungs, but they prepare us to breathe air. Lampreys larvae, a little shy crea-ture, burrow narrow tubes in the soft mud of the ocean floor and live inside comfortably. They feed and breathe happily by pump-ing water through their bodies; they brilliantly absorb the nutri-ents available in the seawater. But sometimes, they shudder in fear when their sweet, tiny home gets clogged by mud and debris and changes into a toxic gas chamber. Their metabolic waste, carbon dioxide, accumulates in the narrow tube and diffuses easily into the water. As the carbon dioxide concentrations keep increasing in the tube, they expel the water accumulated by strong cough-like behavior controlled by a rhythm generator in their brain. This carbon dioxide rhythm generator is the key to the evolution of the lungs.

Neuroscientist Michael Harris and his University of Alaska Fair-bank team recorded videos showing the difference between gill ventilation and a lamprey cough. They removed the brain, found neural activity patterns resembling breathing, and found that the rhythm generator was sensitive to carbon dioxide. Thus, the evo-lution of lung breathing may be a repurposing of carbon diox-ide-sensitive coughs that already existed in lungless vertebrates, like lamprey.

The sensory mode for determining the concentration of gasses in the blood is essential for efficient breathing, and it differs between fish and tetrapods. The primary sensory mode for controlling the breathing rate in fish is achieved by monitoring the oxygen levels by the receptors of the gills. There are always some exceptions; few fish have some peripheral receptors for tracking the carbon dioxide levels. When the pharyngeal gill slits for filter feeding were retasked to gill ventilation, the carbon dioxide rhythm generator was retained to give a nice water wash to clear the delicate gill morphology from external debris.

The stimulus for breathing is not the requirement of oxygen, but the necessity for expelling the carbon dioxide in the blood. If the carbon dioxide levels in the blood increase, it will react with the water molecules to form carbonic acid, lowering the blood pH. This stimulates the chemoreceptors in the brain stem and activates the respiratory muscles, signaling them to increase respiration. The truth is simple: the urge to breathe is the urge to expel carbon dioxide. The evolution converted a strong cough into a simple water wash, then to a rhythm of breathing, dancing to the tune of life.

## EPIC SAGA OF BREATH

Lungs and gills do their job perfectly, but under only one condition: the medium. Air and water are the two mediums for breathing. Due to the different physicochemical properties of water and air, gills and lungs evolved accordingly to suit their medium. Even though lungs are designed to extract oxygen from the air, the secret of origin lies in the ocean. Lungs should have originated in at least the last common ancestor of ray-finned fishes and lobe-finned fishes, which may be in the late Silurian period. Presently, more than 370 air-breathing fish species are in the world; the numbers would have been much higher earlier because the organisms that survive today and have ever evolved in this mighty world are just 0.1%. The first air-breathing vertebrates were fish like lobefin, Silurian sharks, lungfish, etc. The basic lung design of all higher vertebrates is taken from lungfish.

The book's view of the evolution of the lung is a tale of adoption and necessity. As the fish grew in size with its heavy armor and bones, they weighed a lot. To avoid drowning, they must swim constantly, a high-energy-demanding job. When nature tunes and calibrates the energy requirement, it prefers to use it carefully because these resources are acquired with great effort. There was a need for buoyancy. Swim bladders were developed as an extrusion of the air-filled gut wall. Swim bladder helps fish to float like a cloud in the sky. Later on, the oxygen-poor conditions that prevailed in the aquatic habitats, such as rivers and lagoons, especially during seasonal droughts, proved gills inadequate for breathing, and fishes developed blood vessels around the swim bladder and started to extract the oxygen from the air in it. Thus, the lung originated. In his book *On the Origin of Species,* Charles Darwin remarked that the lung in the air-breathing vertebrates had derived from a more primitive swim bladder as a specialized form of respiration.

Our ancestor heroes, like magicians, swam out of the water and walked to the land by converting their fins to limbs and gills to lungs. But in evolution, nothing is magic. Our fish ancestors, who lived 50 million years before they touched the land, possessed the genetic codes for limb-like organs and capabilities for air-breathing needed for that great landing. The recent research paper published in Cell on genomic mapping covering all major early divergent lineages of ray-finned fishes by Xupeng Bi and the team revealed that the lungs in bichir and alligator gar also function in a similar manner and express the same set of genes as human lungs.

The study confirms that, as Darwin predicted, the lungs and swim bladder are identical in gene expression and are homologous organs. However, the contradiction is that it is more likely that the swim bladder evolved from the lungs. According to the research paper, through evolution, one branch of fish might have retained lung functions and be better adapted for air-breathing, eventually leading to the evolution of tetrapods. Other branches of fish modified their lung structures into swim bladders as they started to live in deep waters for bottom feeding where access to air is impossible, enabling them to maintain buoyancy and control pressure changes, enhancing their survival underwater.

## ANCIENT VENTILATOR

Still, one vital question needs to be addressed: why would the lungs evolve if fish had dedicated gills for their oxygen needs? The story continues with another expert. In 1997, Colleen Farmer, Brown University, Rhode Island, proposed an alternative hypothesis for the evolution of lungs. According to Farmer, the lungs were developed as a heart-supporting system.

In pre-vertebrates, life was simple. They absorbed oxygen directly through the skin. The oxygen-poor blood returning from the muscles gets nourished with oxygen on its way to the heart. This process took care of the heart and gave it a steady oxygen supply. But as evolution introduced committed gills capable of extracting oxygen more efficiently from water, it became a party in the water world. These gill-breathing organisms became more active, and their bodies demanded more oxygen. But gills forgot to oxygenate the heart. The oxygenated blood from the gills directly flows to the body tissue, and the heart is the last organ to receive the oxygenated blood due to its two-chambered structure. Sometimes, even worse, there may not be any oxygen left for the heart to feed on.

The heart's function became more complex day by day. They collected the deoxygenated blood from all over the body and pumped it to the gills to replenish it with oxygen. This oxygenated blood flows from the gills to the rest of the body. With the decline of cutaneous respiration and reliance on gill respiration, oxygen supply to the heart diminished. This was problematic, especially during periods of active metabolism when oxygen demand was high. Skeletal muscles consume vast amounts of oxygen, leading to a drop in blood pH, a condition known as acidosis. This acidosis inhibited cardiac function and decreased the affinity of oxygen to hemoglobin, affecting the efficiency of oxygen loading by the gills. The ancestral heart, spongy and lacking blood vessels, suffocated.

Lungs evolved as a lifelong partner; they cared for the heart, providing a steady oxygen supply. With utmost care, lungs, always remember to oxygenate the oxygen-poor blood that returns from muscle to the heart. Lungs made sure that cardiac tissues were now well-oxygenated. Increased cardiac performance supported the active lifestyle and paved the way for developing more complex and diverse life forms capable of exploring the land.

Lungs took its avatar as a supplement to gill ventilation, but in some fish, it superseded the gills. These fishes became loyal air breathers, even in well-oxygenated water with reduced gills. As Theodosius Dobzhansky said, *"Nothing in biology makes sense except in the light of evolution."* In low oxygen conditions, physiologically better gills with suitable capillaries and a thin exchange barrier will diffuse the oxygen from the blood to the oxygen-starved water. Fishes can't be doomed for a long time. They are brilliant enough to prevent oxygen leakage by reducing the gills' physiology.

## AMPHIBIANS

> *"We are rag dolls made out of many ages and skins, changelings who have slept in wood nests, and hissed in the uncouth guise of waddling amphibians. We have played such roles for infinitely longer ages than we have been human. Our identity is a dream. We are processed, not reality."* - Loren Eiseley

To breathe air, fish rise to the surface, exhale through the mouth, inhale, and dive forward. Or they rise to the surface to breathe and reverse into the water. Some curious minds from the ocean saw the land, sipping the fresh air, and dreamed of freely walking on the shores of land devoid of enemies. Competition in the water world is creating devastation, filled with dangerous predators with sharp teeth. There is no hiding place, and it is already crowded. Land with its mesmerizing calmness and alluring beauty, our ancestors had no option but to heed its inner call. The promise of new opportunities was immense, like untapped resources, and challenges were many, as were the rewards. This evolutionary leap forever changed the course of life on Earth.

In the late Paleozoic era, around 542-251 million years, the oxygen concentration was a maximum of 35% and then dropped to 15% within 120 million years. These global hyperoxic conditions fueled the inner courage that led to the vertebrate invasion of land during the Devonian period of 397-416 million years. Elpistostegids, an extinct sarcopterygian fish, are the closest sister group of tetrapods. The changeover from Elpistostegids- tetrapods could have occurred during this period. In the early stages, tetrapods are primarily aquatic animals taking short sunbathes on sandy beaches. Their changed status as land dwellers came with a distinct and evolved look, reflecting their ability to adapt and flourish in this new world.

The sea levels were relatively low in the Devonian period. Shallow marine regions were well-oxygenated. This higher oxygen level throughout the ocean helped the organisms to grow in size with higher metabolic rates. These regions were suitable for the evolution of tetrapods; they learned to crawl and take their first baby steps walking on the seafloor for bottom feeding with their fleshy lobed fins. This power walk helped in the formation and strengthening of limbs. This gave greater mobility, flexibility, digits, and good skeletal support. Walking is energetically less expensive than swimming. Evolution is always very stingy in terms of energy. It loves to conserve energy rather than spend it lavishly.

## ROSE THE FISH OUT OF WATER

The first land invaders were microbes, and then came plants, creeping into the land some 450 million years ago. These were followed by arthropods and a few brave mollusks, which became land snails. Rose: a nine-foot-long crocodile-headed fish Tiktaalik roseae, a 375 million-year-old species, took its first courageous step to land. In 2004, fossils of rose were dug from the grounds of Ellesmere Island in the Canadian Arctic.

Rose represents the transition of life from water to land with its hybrid aquatic and terrestrial traits. This fossil fills the evolutionary link between fish and the first animal that walked out of water. Rose was at the cusp of the fish-tetrapod transition and has a skull, a neck, ribs, and parts of limbs that are similar to four-legged animals known as tetrapods, as well as fish-like features such as a primitive jaw, fins, and scales. Roses are bimodal breathers; they use the gills for aquatic activities and the lungs for aerial respiration. They have eyes on top of their head and live in shallow water.

The spiracular tract is a hole that allows fishes to breathe while eating; in fish that breathe water, the spiracle is seen on the side of the face, whereas in the fish that breathe air, the spiracle is seen on the top. In rose, the spiracles are at an angle between the side and the top, suggesting the presence of both gills and lungs. Tiktaalik can chomp down on its prey like a tetrapod and can suck prey from water like an aquatic creature. They can swim in shallow water, and their strong fins, like legs, can support their movement on land.

Rose the fish out of water, a species with supernatural powers. It tricked big, monstrous predators by disappearing from water and mocking them, happily feasting on land resources like plants and insects.

## TRANSITION

In bimodal breathers, where both gills and lungs are present, they divide their duty; they use the lungs to obtain oxygen from the air and the gills to eliminate carbon dioxide through the water. Over time, the tetrapods lost their spiracular tract; instead, nostrils developed for air breathing. They lost their gills while exploring deep into the land, where continued water access was impossible.

However, tetrapods suffered due to the loss of gills, and this change from bimodal breathers to pure lung respiration created more chaos. At this stage, the lungs had perfected the art of inhaling but were still novice exhalers—a more than sufficient limitation to contribute to the chaos. The consequences of gill loss were the increased concentration of toxic waste like CO2 and nitrogen, which were unable to be excreted from the body, causing an imbalance in the pH levels, water balance, respiratory control, etc... until the lungs mastered the art of exhaling the great mentor skin came for the rescue. By shedding the aquatic scales, they became extremely thin to facilitate the elimination of carbon dioxide, thereby preventing acidosis. Skin helped until lung expertise exhalation.

As the lungs started to inhale oxygen gracefully and exhale carbon dioxide with ease, the skin changed its role from that of a mentor to that of a savior. The skin was covered with hardened scale-protecting tetrapods, which helped minimize water loss. This helped the animals to stay away from the water for an extended period. The kidneys also took over some responsibilities like ion regulation, pH maintenance, and nitrogen elimination as urea.

Among air-breathing vertebrates, amphibians have the simplest and basic form of lungs, which are adequate for cold-blooded and low-metabolism animals. Most of these animals spend their larval and tadpole stages in the aquatic environment, where they depend on the gills. They hatch from jelly-like eggs that must be laid in the water to avoid drying out. Although they are terrestrial organisms, they need water or a moist environment for survival. They produce mucus to keep their skin moist. If they get too dry, they will die.

The transition from ocean to land exposed the gas exchange organs to an environment rich in oxygen; thus, the requirement for ventilation was reduced drastically. At the adult stage, breathing was carried out with the help of the lungs, skin, and mouth. Most amphibians breathe and have specialized skin that allows them to absorb oxygen directly from the water through cutaneous respiration. Reliance on skin breathing limited body size due to negative scaling of surface-area-to-volume ratio.

They don't have chest wall ribs or diaphragm, so breathing through the lungs forces amphibians to swallow air and create pressure changes in the lungs. This is called buccal pumping. They learned this technique from fish who gulp water to breathe, feed, and blow water to disturb the prey. Amphibians can meet their oxygen needs underwater if they are at rest. However, they need to surface for air if they work hard. Some amphibians, like adult lungless salamanders, don't have both lungs and gills; they depend on the skin for the respiration requirements.

The concentration of oxygen levels is highly different in air and water. In air, it is 21%, and in water, it is less than 3% for an equal volume of air, decreasing with water temperature and depth. The concentration of dissolved oxygen in the water is just 1/30th that of air. The water is 1000 times denser and 50 times more viscous than air. This makes water breathing hard and requires more energy than air-breathing to extract an equivalent amount of oxygen. The difference in the oxygen concentrations in the two mediums and the differences in the gas exchange capacity gave a proportionate advantage for tetrapods with an increased oxygen exchange capacity. The gradual progression from water-breathing to air-breathing was associated with a decline in metabolism, so low breathing flow rates can be maintained.

With its motherly care, the ocean gave birth and nurtured life on its lap. Like an ambitious father, Land took life on its shoulder to touch the sky. In this epic journey from water to land, amphibians played a crucial role in bridging the gap in evolution. Their innovations and courage are why we thrive in today's diverse landscape.

## IMPLICATION

- The advantages of tetrapod gill loss include increased head mobility, hearing development, and more. The gills are converted to the ear bones.

- Many of the medicines we use today to fight everything

from AIDS to cancer originate as a toxin in amphibian skin.

- Tiktaalik has primitive versions of the human skull, nostrils, shoulders, neck, and hands.

# REPTILES

*"Reptiles and amphibians are sometimes thought of as primitive, dull and dimwitted. In fact, of course, they can be lethally fast, spectacularly beautiful, surprisingly affectionate and very sophisticated."* - David Attenborough

Rainforests dominated the world, and amphibians were the most common land animals. As the separate land masses collided to form the supercontinent Pangaea, the earth witnessed drying, especially away from the coastlines. Inland regions turned into arid plains and deserts. Rainforest collapse was like salt in the wound; amphibians became more localized to the water for survival. As amphibians depended on water bodies to lay eggs and prevent their skin from drying out, they had no time or might to explore dry habitats far from water bodies. 350 million years ago, during the Carboniferous era, some of them shed their dual life and attained the status of invincible landlords. Animals that could lay water-containing shelled eggs, the amniotes, as we call them, saw a boost in diversity.

The earliest amniotes were small, agile, and lizard-like creatures, and they invented pure air-breathing, self-sustainable large yolk-laden shelled egg that could be laid on land with an amniotic sac containing fluid in which embryo could develop to an advanced stage, capable of fending for itself when hatched. Once soft and delicate skin transformed from a gas exchanger into armor, protecting against dehydration. This new armor took the form of epidermal scales or dermal bone plates. They developed a monolithic skull for better movement and flexibility. Limbs started getting strong and developed claws. Their success story was complete when they learned to optimize their lungs for respiration without outside help. They relied purely on lung breathing.

Their adaptations for terrestrial living were so perfect that they ruled the world not for one or two million years but for 100 million years during the Mesozoic era, often called the Age of Reptiles.

They developed their locomotor capabilities, and their lungs provided the oxygen to support these high metabolic activities. The structure of the gas exchanger is superficially similar to that of lungfish. Amniotes gas exchangers range from simple, single-chambered organs to highly complex multi-chambered and branched lungs and transitional types covering almost everything in between.

The fossil records of Lepidosauromorphs, which are less than 3 cm, show miniature multi-chambered lungs, which resulted in extremely tiny spaces. Multi-chambered lungs have a large surface area and high pulmonary compliance, which provides an advantage for efficient respiration in terrestrial environments. This was pivotal for their success on dry land.

## BEHIND THE BARS

Fish use muscles in their head to pump water over their gills. The first land animals utilized a similar technique, buccal pumping. Modern frogs still use their head and throat to force air into their lungs.

Another major transformation in vertebrate evolution took place; they shifted breathing from the head to the torso. Longer necks evolved. It provided more space for the development of a sophisticated trachea and allowed for a greater volume of air to be moved in and out of the lungs. Necks also contributed to breathing by separating the skull from the ribs. Early tetrapods and amphibians had short necks, and their ribs were closely connected to the skull. This connection limited the mobility of their heads and the expansion of their rib cages, which in turn constrained their breathing. This great separation helped in the evolution of rib breathing.

In reptiles and mammals, the ribs expand to create a space in the chest that draws in breath. Researchers always have a curious mind when we use treadmills for physical development; John Capano and Elizabeth Brainerd at Brown University have different uses. They recorded CT scans and X-ray videos of lizards, Argentines, and tegus strolling on treadmills. They observed the mechanics of rib movements.

Their findings revealed that the ribs' motion during locomotion closely mirrors the patterns involved in breathing. The researchers proposed that the evolution of rib movements and increased joint mobility initially enhanced stride length, stabilized the thorax, or prevented the ribs from bunching together as the animals bent their bodies. Over time, early amniotes adapted these rib movements to occur on both sides simultaneously, allowing for the expansion and contraction of the trunk necessary for inhalation and exhalation. This suggests that rib movements evolved to aid locomotion and were later co-opted to facilitate breathing.

Not only the rib cage but also the intercostal muscles evolved as experts in postural control and locomotion rather than respiratory movements. Initially used by ancestral fish for swimming, these muscles later evolved into the primary muscles for breathing in terrestrial animals. Axial muscles, which run along the sides of the body, including intercostal muscles, first help in exhalation, thereby efficiently pushing the air out of the lungs. Inhalation, on the other hand, was initially accomplished through buccal pumping. As amniotes evolved, these axial muscles adapted to facilitate inhalation too. This coordination allowed tetrapods to maintain a more stable and efficient breathing process during movement. Contrary to the traditional view, several species of lizards still depend on buccal pumps as a last resort to augment coastal aspiration during exercise.

# BEEFY DIAM

The contribution of our reptile ancestors to the development of our lungs does not stop here; the main one is giving a beefy friend a diaphragm. In jawed vertebrates, paired protrusions known as nephric folds develop towards the coelomic cavity—a body cavity that houses internal organs like the digestive system, heart, and lungs. Usually, reptiles use a jacket of muscles to squeeze the ribcage for ventilation, but in some lineages, the nephric folds fuse to form a complete subdivision called intracoelomic septa. Muscle fibers evolved on the edges or throughout the intra-coelomic septum in reptiles like turtles and crocodiles. These muscles, known as diaphragmaticus muscles, are not true diaphragms but serve a similar function in aiding respiration.

With the evolution of calcified eggs, the need to lay them, pee, and poop mandated an increase in energy demands. Moreover, the necessity to facilitate the venous return of blood to the heart elevated the need to generate more efficient positive pressure. But *"Every action has an equal and opposite reaction."* True, the creation of positive pressure also resulted in the creation of negative pressure, which caused the movement of digestive organs into the chest, hampering the expansion of the lungs. International borderlines were made to resolve the dispute by muscularizing the proto-diaphragm.

The diaphragm's primary function is ventilation, particularly at rest, which is not the primary driver in its evolution. Indeed, the diaphragm's inspiratory role may be an exaptation or "side-effect" of its original development. The current need is to separate the larger coelomic cavity into separate thoracic and abdominal cavities, creating room for internal organs.

This is further proved by the studies conducted with engineered mice so that specific cells would glow inside mouse embryos and then be tracked as they multiplied and migrated. The diaphragm originates from the esophagus as a sheet in two separate waves. In the first wave, a sheet of connective tissue separates the big chambers into the abdominal and thoracic cavities. Scientists suspect embryonic mutations played a part in developing this connective tissue sheet. The second task is simple: Once the connective tissue cells make a template, muscle cells follow the chemical trail left by the connective tissue. Muscles form a sandwich layer, creating a breathing pump.

So, did the diaphragm develop in mammals or reptiles? Diaphragm is a trademark trait of mammals, whereas reptiles lack a true diaphragm. A fossil diaphragm probably will never be found simply due to its bad chances of becoming preserved. Hence, it should be deduced with the functional approximations.

Evolution sometimes produces bizarre-looking creatures and incorporates novel innovations to make them survive, the fruits we enjoy now. Around 300-250 million years ago, during the Permian period, Caseidae, large sedentary grazers similar to our cow, lived in the Paleozoic era. They are mammal-like reptiles with barrel-shaped trunks, short necks, tiny heads, hampered rib mobility, and unusual joints. These features are more than enough to gravely impair the inhalation capacity.

They love water and have a predominantly aquatic life. They enjoy diving in water in search of food and mates. These lifestyles require them to surface regularly to have lungs full of air. However, their features are not enough for a realistic adaptation to such an environment and habit, not if it had an auxiliary motor like the diaphragm. The closest living relatives of caseids are the mammals. The research concludes that the least common ancestor of caseids and mammals already had a diaphragm more than 300 million years ago–about 50 million years earlier than previously assumed.

Plato and Aristotle viewed the heart as the soul and the diaphragm as the seat of the soul, which separates the abdominal cavity and protects the heart. Reptilian lungs tend to be larger than mammalian lungs. Due to the increased surface area and low diameter, it is difficult to inflate the lungs. Drawing air into the lungs creates a suction or negative pressure within the thoracic cavity. This negative pressure is achieved by expanding the thoracic cavity, primarily through the diaphragm and intercostal muscles. The diaphragm's role is multifunctional, from breathing to digestion and stability to emotional state regulation.

Reptiles' innovations, ranging from the development of rib movements that facilitated both locomotion and respiration to the emergence of diaphragmatic muscles, have laid the foundation for the complex respiratory systems seen in mammals. Their contributions have allowed for more efficient breathing and enabled the diverse forms of life we see today to thrive in various environments.

## IMPLICATIONS

- The diaphragm produces very high abdominal pressures, which help human eves give birth to infants with disproportionately larger brains.

- The diaphragm helped mammals to evolve warm-blooded metabolism.

- The alveoli could not have evolved without the diaphragm because the high surface tension would have collapsed the alveoli.

- A spasm in the diaphragm causes a hiccup. In fish, the nerves that activate breathing take a short journey from the brain to the throat and gills. In us, the signals are more complicated to reach far down to the chest and diaphragm. Unfortunately, anything interfering with one of these nerves can block their function or cause a spasm.

- The primary ventilatory function of the rib cage in mammals is to prevent the collapse of the thoracic wall when the diaphragm contracts and decreases thoracic pressure.

## BIRDS

*"A bird is an instrument working according to mathematical law, which instrument it is within the capacity of man to reproduce with all its movements, but not*

*with a corresponding degree of strength, though it is deficient only in the power of maintaining equilibrium. We may therefore say that such an instrument constructed by man is lacking in nothing except the life of the bird, and this life must needs be supplied from that of man."* — Leonardo da Vinci

From an old emperor, a complete air-breathing reptile, born two beautiful little princesses independently around the same time. One ruled the land-named mammals, and the other ruled the sky-named birds. They both used this new skill of aerobic respiration to its maximum potential and evolved tremendously. They have more similarities as siblings, especially in their cardiovascular, renal, gastrointestinal, endocrine, and nervous systems. Also, there is some disparity in reproduction, feeding, bones, etc. Our interest lies evidently in their respiratory system, which is drastically different in terms of the morphology and structure of gas exchangers. This difference arose due to the increased demand for energy and metabolic needs, with the divergent locomotion modes demanding higher breathing rates.

## KISSING THE CLOUDS

Recently discovered fossils from China, South America, and other countries speak volumes about a crazy dream of a small meat-eating theropod dinosaur in the late Jurassic world around 150 million years ago. They dreamed of gliding in the air, kissing the clouds, and touching the sky. These little dinos were not meant to be birds. The unique features of birds, such as feathers and flight, developed gradually through many small steps and served various purposes over time. Feathers, for example, initially helped with temperature regulation and later adapted for flight. The forelimbs of early dino lengthened and evolved into long wings with feathers that helped warm and protect their eggs. At the same time, hind limbs are shortened and refined flight control. Each step in their evolution added new functions, leading to the diverse and specialized birds we see today. The features of birds are slowly ingrained in them through these minor adaptations, helping them realize their dreams.

This newfound freedom to fly made them a successful species that helped them to prosper and survive. They viewed the earth from different angles at a superior point, which helped them find and catch their prey easily. They used big trees as their home, played hide and seek with the predators, and always emerged victorious. Due to their lifestyle, their metabolic rates were very high, and their energy demands were skyrocketing to fuel their dreams of flight. This created a need for efficient gas exchangers, and true to it, among the gas exchangers, the bird's respiratory system is the most complex and efficient lung-air sac system prevailing to date. Remember that they lack a diaphragm, and their lungs are closely attached to the ribs.

## A TWEET BREATHE

Their lungs are superior due to the smooth flow of air in and out of their body. Birds' lungs have a cross-current gas exchange system with continuous, unidirectional airflow. This arrangement helps birds by providing continuous oxygen and maximizing the oxygen they can take from the air. The air enters through the nose and moves through the trachea, air sacs, and then through the lungs, where the gas exchange occurs, then to the anterior air sac, which will ultimately be expelled out during exhalation. Here, air sacs play a crucial role in maintaining the continuous unidirectional flow of air; they do not participate in the gas exchange but act as a temporary reservoir of air. This unidirectional airflow maximizes the rapid gas exchange and ensures a constant oxygen supply to the tissues and organs. It also keeps the lungs compact and virtually constant during breathing. The inspiratory and expiratory muscles help in inhalation and exhalation, respectively.

The lung's efficiency mainly influences the birds' flight capacity. The birds with a higher metabolic rate have superior lungs to those with low metabolic birds. They tweaked the efficiency of the lungs by introducing a cross-current exchange method. The flow of blood and air in the blood capillary and air capillary are opposite in direction; this arrangement facilitates maximum oxygen uptake even at flight in high altitudes, which is impractical for others. The hypoxic conditions at high altitudes stimulate the arterial chemoreceptors to increase the breath rate. It also adjusts by decreasing the body temperature and dropping the birds' metabolic requirements, saving them energy to fly high for long hours.

The hemoglobin of birds has a higher oxygen affinity, which augments their capacity to transport oxygen. It is a game changer, especially at high altitudes with low oxygen availability. Avian lungs are relatively small, which helps reduce the weight of the respiratory system and helps in the flight of the birds. Even the cold exposure does not cause respiratory distress. Birds use 2.5 to 3 times more oxygen than mammals running fast on the ground. For example, the Ruooells griffon vulture can fly up to 37000 ft., which we can't imagine. These features enabled the birds to conquer the skies and thrive in diverse habitats worldwide.

With constant innovation and tweaking, birds perfected the art of breathing, developing one of the most efficient respiratory systems in the animal kingdom. This enables them to soar at altitudes where oxygen is scarce. Their adaptation fueled their incredible endurance and symbolized the evolutionary creativity that has allowed birds to conquer the skies. The avian breath proves nature's ability to innovate and optimize, allowing it to inhabit nearly every corner of the Earth.

## IMPLICATIONS

- At sea level, carbon dioxide is the primary stimulus for ventilation. At high altitudes, hypoxia increases ventilation significantly when the oxygen pressure decreases around 3000 m.

- Hypoxia acts as a vasodilator in the systemic circulation, but it is a vasoconstrictor in the pulmonary circulation.

- If the mammalian lung were replaced with the avian lung, a person would ascend 780 m higher for the same arterial blood gasses.

- The avian lung is not a prerequisite for flying. Bats are

excellent flyers, cover long distances, and tolerate extreme hypoxia with a mammalian lung. However, they cannot fly at high altitudes and lose heat in hypothermic conditions.

## MAMMALS

*" [On seeing the marsupials in Australia for the first time and comparing them to placental mammals:] An unbeliever ... might exclaim, "Surely two distinct Creators must have been at work. "* — Charles Darwin

Lush green earth with bustling life and scenic beauty had crumbled to ashes in one of the biggest environmental catastrophes in Earth's history. About 252 million years ago, in the Permian period, massive volcanoes spewed up from the gut of Mother Earth and flooded Siberia. 2.7 million square miles of lava, an area nearly as large as Australia, and feverishly hot ocean surface waters potentially reaching more than 104 degrees Fahrenheit. These eruptions lasted more than 2 million years and perished more than 96 percent of marine creatures and 70 percent of land species. It was the biggest trap that was laid down to kill life on the earth and aptly named the Siberian trap.

A lucky few escaped these traps to flourish on the earth with life; one among them was Cynodont, our grandmother. They are Mammal-like reptiles from the late Triassic period about 235 million years ago. They looked like scaly rats, smaller than a loaf of bread, roaming through the dangerous Brazilian jungle, hunting for small insects. Like most mammals, they had mammal-like skulls and jaws but still laid eggs. Shortly, within 5 to 10 million years, something gigantic, fearsome predator of this earth was developing in the womb of Mother Earth: Dinosaurs.

## RAGS TO RICHES

Mammals may be one of the most ferocious organisms in the current world, with lions, tigers, bears, and even deadlier humans. But the situation was different then. It was a world dominated by dinosaurs. Cynodonts gave rise to mammals named Morganucodontids. Morgi, a tiny shrew-sized creature, lived in the shadows of the dinosaurs. Dino ruled the earth ruthlessly like devils; mammals were nothing but the lunch for those dinos' big bellies. Morgi and other mammalian lineages that evolved around that time were timid; they preyed on insects in the dark to ensure dinos slept. The dominance of dinosaurs ensured that our mammalian ancestors remained no larger than a cat.

These little guys were so active they fed on insects and had to get every calorie they could from what they ate. They developed jaws and teeth to process the food in their mouths, which gave them more energy. Morgi developed something special within her body, the world's first mammary gland; she safely nursed her pups in the dark burrows hiding from the dangerous monsters. She doesn't have nipples for her pups to hang on, but they happily slurped her wet fur around her belly, which secreted water, salts, and proteins to feed her newborns to keep them survive. Morgi is a caring mother. If not, her lineage will die out, which is the true mammalian trait we still possess deep in our subconscious.

66 million years ago, in the last Mesozoic period, the fate of the earth, the mammals, and dinosaurs changed. It was an asteroid or comet, who knows, but it punched a hole in the face of Earth with a speed of more than 25 kilometers per second and impacted the Earth at the tip of the Yucatan platform. The enormous amount of energy this impact generates was equivalent to a hundred teratons of TNT, more than one billion Hiroshima. Several hundred billion tons of carbon dioxide, sulfur dioxide, and water vapor were injected into the Earth's atmosphere. The ashes and the dust it threw into the sky blocked the sun's rays, decreasing or stopping the photosynthesis. Herbivores died, and carnivores followed them to their graves. Ash was raining back to the earth copiously, making heaps of soot. The climate was volatile, with tsunamis, wildfires, earthquakes, and volcanic eruptions. When it finally stabilized, almost everything was dead. The most extraordinary beast of all time was charred to death, and with it, more than 50% of Earth's fauna and flora on land and in the ocean vaporized.

The legacy of dinos ended tragically; only a handful of small birds flew, carrying on the tales of dinosaurs to the present day. Creatures who were small enough or burrowed deep enough to hide escaped the catastrophe. Mammals were waiting for the right time and place to be resurrected and adore the throne like a pharaoh. Death created an opportunity. Survivors occupied the vacant spaces elegantly.

Only 7% of mammals survived, but they diversified into many forms within a few million years. There are 4500 different species of mammals living in almost every environment on earth, including the oceans, freshwater, on and below the ground, in the treetops, and even in the sky. Mammals winning the survival race seized the crown from the dinosaurs and ruled the world to date. On the go, mammalian eves developed placenta and started to incubate their babies within them. The placenta is very expensive for mothers to maintain but is precious. It nourishes and protects the fetus from the mother's immune system. They not only developed in the womb, but also in motherhood. They nurtured, cared and loved their little ones more than themselves, which made mammals a successful species.

Mammals started to create enough heat and control their body temperature. It is like gassing the car to keep the engines going; we have to take food just to produce enough heat. To eat more, animals must hunt and gather food, spending more energy to stay warm. It is a vicious cycle where mammals use more energy just to get more energy. Elephants, for example, spend most of their day munching to keep them warm. To sustain themselves, they must eat as much as 5% of their body weight daily. To meet the increased energy requirements, mammalian lungs underwent functional and morphological adaptations to cope. Basics are in place by the billions of years of evolution. Now, only minor tweaking here and there is required.

# UPGRADATION

Mammalian lungs took a different track from the bird's lungs. They got their simple and multi-chambered lungs from their reptilian grandfathers and started remodifying them into a more complex one. The principal aim of the mammalian lungs is to find ways and means to increase the gas exchange surface to its maximum in whatever ways possible. It gave birth to Broncho alveolar lungs; the design was inspired by the nature of an inverted airway tree. The high branching of the bronchial system originated slowly with stepwise subdivisions in branched bronchioles and ducts covered with numerous bubble-like sacs known as alveoli. Mammals inhale oxygen-rich air that funnels into smaller branches, ending in tiny sacs where oxygen enters, and carbon dioxide leaves the bloodstream. When mammals exhale, the depleted air follows the same route out of the body, exhibiting a rhythmic pattern like dancing to the tune of rising breasts.

It achieved its goal of increasing the surface area to nearly the size of a tennis court in humans by including 274 to 790 million alveoli. The master stroke was folding this large surface area into a confined chest cavity. Alveoli are gassed by to and fro airflow movements. The problem of supplying oxygen to all points on such a large surface was solved by the evolution of an airway tree with alveoli arranged around the last few branches, looking like a bunch of grapes. The development of the diaphragm and surfactant system was a boon to the lungs; without them, the alveoli could not have evolved because the high surface tension would have collapsed them.

An extensive network of capillaries was formed throughout the lungs to withstand a flood of blood flowing during heavy exercise. It further polished their role by thinning the tissue barrier. It assured the efficient delivery of inspired air to the nook and corner of the lungs. With the uncoupling of respiratory and locomotion functions, the mammalian lineage got the power to the legs for the great leap and ascending of the earth's throne. Here, the savior is the diaphragm, which allows mammals to maintain continuous and efficient ventilation of the lungs, even during strenuous physical activities. This muscle contracts and flattens to increase the thoracic cavity's volume, reducing pressure and allowing air into the lungs. While lungs were evolving as an efficient machine in extracting oxygen, they mastered additional skills apart from respiration. It also participated in immune modulation, production, regulation, and metabolism of pharmacologically active factors like serotonin, adrenaline, noradrenaline, regulation of heat dissipation, and water conservation.

Mammals, like successful athletes in a relay race, handed the baton of evolution to humans with great care and precision. Through countless generations, they have honed the art of breathing and adapting to diverse environments and challenges. In each breath we take, we should honor the millions of years of evolution that brought us here—a journey that began in the depths of ancient oceans, passed through countless species, and is still evolving.

# CHAPTER 6

# HUMAN BREATH

*"If the germ plasm wants to swim in the ocean, it makes itself a fish; if the germ plasm wants to fly in the air, it makes itself a bird. If it wants to go to Harvard, it makes itself a man. The strangest thing of all is that the germ plasm that we carry around within us has done all those things. There was a time, hundreds of millions of years ago, when it was making fish. Then ... amphibia ... reptiles ... mammals, and now it's making men." — George Wald*

Before deep diving into the human breath and its minute transformations, which our hominin ancestors underwent, let's see a small trailer of our evolution. In his book The Descent of Man, Charles Darwin speculated that it was "probable" that Africa was the cradle of humans because our two closest living relatives—chimpanzees and gorillas—live there. But in the early 20th century, the world believed humans evolved somewhere in

Eurasia. However, a fossilized skull mold from South Africa in 1924 made anatomists rethink their earlier views. Almost 3 million years ago, a hungry crown eagle plucked a 3.3-year-old child from the ground, carried it to be eaten, and dropped him into a hole. He was named Taung Child, and his fossils revolutionized and challenged the views of human evolution. After 20 years, scientists accepted the importance of Africa as a significant source of human evolution. Although we belong to different countries with well-defined borders and diverse cultures, the truth is our hometown is Africa: the cradle of humankind. Seven million years ago, a female ape gave birth to two daughters. One is the great granny of chimpanzees, and the other is our granny.

## FLASHBACK

Sahelanthropus tchadensis, known as Toumai, lived close to the breakup event 6 to 7 million years ago between hominines and apes. Toumai is the closest to the evolutionary branching event. With predominant ape-like features, he tried taking the baby steps of walking.

About 4.4 million years ago, Ardipithecus Ramidus was born from them. Ardi mastered walking to some extent.

Then comes our Southern Ape Lucy, generically called Australopithecus Afarensis, whose fossil was found in Ethiopia and Tanzania 3.85 - 2.95 million years ago. Their body plan and lifestyle work well; they are the longest-lived hominin species. They happily swing through the trees, climbing, foraging, and walking briskly.

A clever Homo habilis, known as the "handyman," emerged around 2.4 million years ago. He was a master of early stone tools. His larger brain and ability to shape stones into useful implements marked a significant leap in cognitive skills, and his tools helped him hunt, forage, and protect himself.

Then came Homo erectus 1.89 million years ago, the erect ape-man. He is a man of upright posture with human-like body proportions, with shorter arms and longer legs relative to his torso. Mastery of fire provided warmth, protection, and a way to cook food, contributing to better nutrition and allowing bigger brains to evolve. Some decided to leave their homeland and settle in North Africa, Europe, and Asia. They crossed scorching deserts and climbed high mountains. From the plains of Africa to the icy tundras of Siberia, they left their mark. The human population evolved in different directions, adapting to every challenge they encountered. As a result, several distinct species arose.

Humans in Europe and western Asia are named Homo Neanderthals, known as Neanderthals. They adapted to the region's cold climates with compact, massive musculature. They co-existed with homo sapiens. Their brains are larger than ours.

Homo sapiens present humans known as wise men evolved around 2 lakh years ago. They are the only surviving human species. Sapiens found they could control the growth and breeding of certain plants and animals; thus, they mastered farming and herding animals. At last, they stopped wandering and settled down, demarking their boundaries according to their will and might, dividing the whole world into bits and pieces.

There are around 20 different hominin species that are part of our family tree. For the past 7 million years, our ancestors have shared the planet with other hominins. Just 300,000 years ago, at least nine species of humans wandered the earth simultaneously. Recent research proves that hominins had extensive and regular sexual intercourse between them. But somehow, we sapiens are the last humans standing out of a large, diverse group of hominins. Did a better infant survival rate and tolerance towards extreme climatic conditions help us survive? Or, as a short-tempered species, we would have done an ethnic cleansing? What happened is a riddle, but the truth is for about 12000 years, homo sapiens are alone on this earth. Did others die, or are they still with us in some way?

## MARCH PAST

Earlier, the big brain was considered a unique character that made us hominins. But the truth is that the burning desire to stand tall is what made us humans. Fossil records prove walking upright came before big brains in the story of human evolution. Viewing the world from a different angle gave a different perspective on life and slowly but steadily assisted humankind's evolution, leading them to the pinnacle of the world.

Evolution has given adaptations that helped species to climb the top of the life pyramid; humans walking helped them climb that pyramid. Even though not perfectly like we do today, they tried it some 7 million years ago, says a fossil skeleton of Sahelanthropus tchadensis dearly called Toumai. Toumai learned to toddle in

African soil when great African separation was happening—recent isotope studies of soil date the separation to around 6 million years. East Africa gets on its own like a baby separating from its mother and lurching towards the Arabian Sea. Indeed, this separation will take millions of years, but it started creating havoc. The shifting mass of the mantle underneath is an omen for the terrible geological events that will unfold. Earthquakes were a daily event; lava flowed like a flood, the rain became scarce, forests shrunken, and grassy plains opened. At last, the crack was filled with seawater, completing the separation.

In 1871, Charles Darwin explained in his book The Descent of Man that hominids needed to walk on two legs to free up their hands. However, anthropologist C. Owen Lovejoy of Kent State University gave a different explanation due to the climatic conditions that prevailed in Ardi's era, which would have made it more challenging and more time-consuming for individuals to find food, especially for females with children. At this point, the sex trade began. Males gathered food for females and their needy young ones, and in return, females mated exclusively with their providers. For this exclusive joy, males must walk upright and carry food in their arms, freeing them from walking. It is argued that Ardi invented hominin monogamy to make the trade a considerable success. She waited lustfully for her partner to return to her, swapping the handful of food for breading. This hypothesis is further supported by chimpanzees' tendency to walk when carrying rare or valuable foods. Most of the evolution was spearheaded in search of food and to avoid predation, but we humans evolved with an instinct for having more sex. Somewhere deep inside, it strikes a chord.

Another line of thought is females have a greater need for food, considering pregnancy and feeding the young. Female bodies evolved to be smaller than their counterparts; they require fewer calories when they are not pregnant—Eve had to venture further to get food due to the geological changes affecting the food chain. Walking would have been advantageous for carrying food to younger ones and doubly good if she had to take a baby, too. There are around thirty hypotheses for the evolution of walking. Who knows why we started to walk, but it's true it's what made us stand apart from the rest of the world. Walking gave us an edge; it helped us improve our ability to survey our surroundings and detect danger and food at a great distance. They learned to handle tools, defend themselves, and grab food with freeing hands.

## THE CAGE OF LOVE

The rhythm of the heart and lungs always dance according to the speed of the strides taken. Although breathing and walking have different aspects and mechanics, breathing always compliments walking. In quadrupeds, due to their horizontal nature, their thoracic cavities are compressed. This dramatically affects the pressure distribution along the chest cavity. The thoracic cavity expanded vertically when our granny adopted an upright walking posture. The joints in our thoracic spine are so unique that they are tight enough to protect vital organs like the heart and lungs, but loose enough to allow for the movements of breathing. This helped reduce the pressure in the region and allowed the lungs to expand more fully with each inhalation.

Great apes, gorillas, and chimpanzees have longer, deeper, and forward-protruding chest cavities. This structure powers their arms for locomotion, allowing them to swing and climb effortlessly in their tree shed. Our early hominins stood taller. As millions of years passed, their posture became more and more upright, assigning the freed hands new tasks. Along with it, the rib cage, too, silently changed.

Our hominin grandpas had a conical ribcage supported by a more muscular diaphragm than their descendants. This combo allowed them to fully expand their lungs, take deep breaths, and fuel their bodies with the oxygen needed to navigate their world.

As the perfection of their strides improved, their rib cage shifted from a conical shape to a more barrel-like structure. This change supported thoracic breathing, a new form of respiration that involves using the muscles between the ribs and neck to raise and lower the rib cage to pull air into the lungs and push it out. Chest breathing activates accessory respiratory muscles that tighten the neck, chest, and vocal cords and can trigger a fight-or-flight stress reflex. A chest-breathing pattern was more helpful in short bursts when running from danger. There was enough danger for our ancestors to encounter in their primitive world.

Gigantic buddies, Neanderthals, had 20% larger lung capacities than modern humans. Their oxygen consumption was high so that they could maintain the basic metabolism of a heavier body, larger brain, and larger muscles. They achieved this through larger and more powerful rib cages, complementing their larger body mass.

Our pelvis evolved to become shorter and broader. It was a significant disadvantage for our eves during childbirth, but it provided more excellent stability for walking. This restructuring also helped support the internal organs, including the diaphragm, more effectively. The diaphragm moved into a more horizontal position. The diaphragm, a major muscle for breathing, now works more efficiently due to less pressure from the abdominal organs when in an upright position. This new alignment allowed the diaphragm to contract more effectively, increasing lung capacity and improving our breathing. Contrary to it in quadrupeds, the diaphragm has to bear the extra brunt of pressure from the abdominal organs.

The repositioning of the head and neck in bipeds also influenced the structure of the upper airways. The foramen magnum, the opening in the skull through which the spinal cord passes, shifted to a more central position beneath the skull, positioning the head directly above the spine. The human spine transformed from a C-shaped curvature of quadruped into an S-shaped curve with distinct neck, chest, and lower back bends. This curvature helps balance the head over the pelvis, providing stability while standing and walking on two legs. Moreover, the chest is flattened from front to back so that human body weight is concentrated as close to the spine as possible. This realignment reduces the energy needed to maintain an upright stance and helps absorb the shock from walking and running. It also creates a more direct and open airway, reducing the work required for breathing and facilitating better airflow.

Walking was terrific, but it has some negative legacy that is part and parcel of this great gift that defines our humanity. The main villain here is a powerful force created by this mighty universe, named gravity. It always poses a significant challenge to our soft hearts. Gravity can affect the return of blood to the heart from the lower extremities. This can lead to less efficient venous return, potentially impacting cardiac output and, thus, overall oxygen delivery to the body during intense physical activity. The upright posture can significantly lead to blood pressure drops, causing dizziness and possibly fainting. This can momentarily impair effective breathing and oxygen supply to the brain. Gravity also shows its strength to our beefy partner diaphragm. In the upright position, the diaphragm has to work against gravity, particularly during inhalation. This can increase the work of breathing compared to when lying down, where gravity assists the diaphragm's movement. The abdominal organs press down on the diaphragm more significantly, restricting its movement and making deep breathing more challenging.

Despite these minor disadvantages, it has helped our granny take happy strides in the deserts of Africa. The anatomical changes accompanying her footsteps optimized her breathing, improving her survival.

Throughout life's history, our great-grandparents were restless creatures. This eagerness to explore the surroundings was the driving force behind evolution. Our single-celled prokaryotes took the first decision to leave the hydrothermal vents. Then came fishes swimming with their fins. Later, they gathered the courage to step onto the land. From there, some started flying, others began walking, and both were kings of two different worlds. The sky and the land, respectively. Throughout their adventurous travel, breath was their companion. It changed forms according to their needs, helping them to reach their destination. Breath was the loyal partner of these backpackers.

## SELFISH BRAIN

Muscles tense. One leg stands as a pillar, supporting the body upright, while the other acts as a pendulum, swinging from behind. The heel firmly touches down, and the body's weight boldly shifts as the legs reverse position. 3.6 million-year-old hominin footprints from Laetoli and Tanzania prove our hominin ancestors mastered the art of human gait.

What's next? Our hominins took a new powerful tool for their personal growth. It was our brain. For the first few million years as humans, the brains of early hominins did not grow much larger than those of our ape ancestors, but for the last 3 million years, our brains grew fattier, making us the deadliest creature in the world.

A complex brain was a significant advantage to our early folks in their complex world. It helped process and store much information and was a big advantage in their social interactions and encounters with unfamiliar habitats.

Our ancestors wired our brains with 86 billion neurons, 16 billion of which were allocated to the cerebral cortex. Although our brains are tinier than elephants and whales, our cortices are far denser. These 16 billion neurons were the masters of higher-level processes like language, memory, reasoning, thought, learning, decision-making, emotion, intelligence, and personality. Thus, thanks to the brain architect, humans won the race to have the most cortical neurons among any species on Earth.

Throughout human evolution, the brain size tripled. Although our brain is just two percent of our body's weight, it gobbles up 20 percent of our total energy, 20 percent of the oxygen supply, and 20 percent of our blood goes to the brain for nourishment. The muscles were looted to feed this hungry brain, and we lost our muscle mass. When our lineage split from the apes, we were also stronger, like them. Great apes get more power out of their muscles. They feed their muscles rather than their brains.

It is also argued that the invention of cooking was crucial to human evolution. Soft, cooked foods are much easier to digest and delicious to eat than tough, raw ones, yielding more calories to our brain with less gastrointestinal work. With fewer jobs, our intestines shrank, and the energy that nourished these organs was diverted to binge the brain. In short, the art of cooking bloated the brain at the expense of the gut.

Moreover, archaic Juliet's and Romeo's would have lusted for romantic dates from intelligent mates, crowding the prospects for smaller brains. Sexual selection, a powerful tool, gave birth to more jumbo-brainers. Thus, hominins managed to outsmart other species by providing ways to support brains large enough to accommodate all those extra cells.

The large brain stuffed with neurons came at a huge cost. Not only did the brain evolve, but the human skull also became big when most animals found a quiet spot away from the group and gave birth in solitude. On the contrary, we seek assistance during childbirth. The evolution of bigger brains and bipedalism made human birth more difficult and painful for our eves. She needed a helping hand, and thus, the practice of midwifery was born. Midwife can spell the difference between life and death for her and her little baby. What about the impact of the bumpy brain on our breath? The brain not only looted energy from other organs to feed its appetite but also encroached into others' territory and occupied others' estates.

## HUMPY HOOTER

Our nose, a little protruding tunnel, is an evolutionary mystery. Unlike us, in many higher mammals, the nose is a hidden secret protected within the facial bones. The noses of chimpanzees and other great apes like bonobos, gorillas, and orangutans are relatively flat. The early lineage of human Australopithecines had a flat amid facial morphology like our great apes, with no nasal protrusion. Their nasal bones are small and flat with no curvatures and their faces with strong upper and lower jaw protrusions. If we could see our hominin grandfather, we would mistake them as chimpanzees walking on legs with more perfect strides. They securely sheltered their nasal cavity within the facial bones, far from the mechanical forces of the world outside.

In the play of evolution, the hominin skull underwent a dramatic reorganization to accommodate the jumbo brains. As Homo erectus appeared 1.89 million years ago, brains grew and faces became relatively smaller to make room for the newcomer. With no space left, the secret chamber popped out of its den, forming an external protrusion; thus, Homo erectus is the first primate species to develop an externally protruding nose.

The main agenda for the nose is to assist with respiration and a sense of smell, known as olfaction. For a four-legged creature, the soil is just beneath its nose; the olfactory functions are essential for day-to-day survival. But as the man stood tall on his two legs, he distanced himself from the mother earth that lay like a sheet beneath his feet. His bulging nose was adapted like a finely tuned instrument for stereo olfaction. Each nostril, operating independently, sent different signals to the brain, enabling them to pinpoint the direction of odors. This ability was a vital asset in the vast, open landscapes. It aided them in spatial navigation by using multiple senses, like seeing, hearing, and smelling, in brain areas to represent position and help in movement. Even though our olfactory abilities are inferior to other animals like dogs, studies have proven we can accurately follow an odor trail of chocolate across a grassy field.

The protruding human nose increased the accuracy of stereo olfaction, a crucial adaptation for long-distance travel. As Homo erectus and their descendants started to venture beyond the borders of Africa, encountering diverse and unpredictable climates, they eventually settled in the colder climates of Eurasia. Odors were easier to detect in Africa's hot and humid environments, favoring olfaction in such climates. However, more frigid, drier regions are the most stressful for our physical body because these conditions are far from the internal condition of our body, and the nose begins to adapt in other ways.

The geometry of narrow nasal cavities influences the velocity of inhaled air. It helps condition air by increasing the air turbulence and improving contact with the nasal mucosa. As the air swirls inside the nasal cavity, 90% of the air gets conditioned by warming it to body temperature and saturating it with water vapor before it touches the lungs. The long noses serve as front-line defenders against the pathogens. Some studies say it even helps cool the brain. Without a tubular nose, low humid air will dry the mucous, impairing its mucociliary function and will increase respiratory tract infection. European archaic Neanderthals have taller noses than modern humans.

Adams, on average, tend to have wider nares, longer nasal ridges, protruding nasal tips, and more prominent nostrils having a larger surface area than their eves. Choanae are two openings at the back of the nasal passage with a pure respiratory function. Adams with larger choanae had the upper hand against smaller ones in endurance pursuits like hunting, a trait their mates adored, leading to the sexual selection of longer noses. About 15000 years ago, the shift from a nomadic hunting lifestyle to sedentary agriculture diminished the need for olfactory navigation. Instead of navigation, olfaction helped identify diseases, select mates, and cook, which caused a significant increase in nasal height. A narrow nose with some trade-off of stereo olfaction allowed increased sensitivities to odorants, which turned out to be a billion-dollar perfume business worldwide.

## AN EMPTY SPACE

The sinus was the worst affected by brain encroachment. The nose escaped the invading brain by protruding outward, making its own room. Unfortunately, sinuses can't copy the brilliant tactics of the nose because they are just air-filled spaces in the skull, so they accepted their defeat and shrank.

Why sinuses evolved is a mystery. They are suggested to produce mucus and nitrogen oxide to defend against infection, provide thermal and shock protection to the nervous system, and help distribute stress from chewing. It aided in the humidification and warming of the air breathed. The fact is their role and responsibility are not clear. Some think that sinuses are an example of an evolutionary spandrel, a structure that evolved as the by-product of something else and has no initial role. Further adaptation assigned new functions later in the evolutionary time.

In our great apes and early hominins like Tomaui, Ardi, and Lucy, the size and shape of sinuses were directly related to the amount of space available for them to grow. Their baby brain needed only a little space, and the sinuses were large. As hominins learned to walk upright, sinuses helped them by reducing the weight of the skull and balancing the head atop a vertical spine, reducing the energy required for movement.

The story changed track over the last 2 million years. From Homo erectus onwards, our hominins show a wide variation in frontal sinuses. As the baby's brain learned speech, emotion, and planning, it grew in size. As a result, the sinus was compromised.

Why it evolved is a mystery, but its current responsibilities are predictable. What happens if the sinus gets compromised? The answer is clear: It sucks and makes us feel like drainage by blocking the nose, propagating bacteria, and causing a nasty headache. In simple terms, sinuses are traded for the sake of a jumbo brain.

## SYMPHONY OF BREATH

With walking, homo separated from others; with jumbo brains, they dominated others; with speech, they commanded the destruction of others. Speech was the ultimate tool that made us complete.

Our forefathers communicated much like their nonhuman primate cousins—with short, unmodulated utterances like hoots, howls, whistles, barks, etc. Their vocalizations were simple, devoid of intricate patterns and modulations. These early sounds were enough for basic communication but lacked the complexity to convey detailed information or express emotions. Upright humans, with their larger brains, developed speech. When do humans start to speak? The exact timeline is a matter of debate; many scholars agree that Homo erectus laid the groundwork for the sophisticated speech that later evolved.

Around 1.6 to 1 million years ago, Hominins started to develop fine breath control, a crucial prerequisite for the emergence of speech. From simple utterances of sounds to beautiful songs, speech is a marvelous evolution. Speech is unique because it makes us the only animals to express thoughts in words. Language started with people imitating the surrounding sounds, like nature sounds, animal calls, and the sound of tools. To reinforce the idea, our ancestors used gestures like pointing at things, making faces, and imitating actions, fortifying the meaning of the sounds. Eventually, our archaic grandpa developed full sign language with sound utterances. At some point, sounds turned into words, and then these words formed sentences, leaving the gestures useless. Talking out loud was an effective communication tool, even if you couldn't see someone or if he was far away.

Around 50000 years ago, humanity experienced a sudden cultural explosion. They started to build houses, hunting became specialized and sophisticated with stone stools, they learned the art of food storage, etc. Along with these changes, this era witnessed the birth of a full-fledged human language. Our ancestors' ability to share ideas, tell stories, and build complex social structures was a remarkable leap. Many cognitive and physical features have undergone drastic changes to achieve this milestone. At the heart of this linguistic evolution was the role of breath control.

When compared to our predecessors, Australopithecines and Homo ergaster, the thoracic vertebral canal had increased in size in modern humans and Neanderthal. This enlargement indicated a greater nerve supply to the thoracic muscles, which controlled the intercostal and abdominal muscles essential for fine-tuning our breath. This anatomical adaptation allowed our ancestors to manage their breath precisely, producing a steady airflow and varying sounds necessary for speech.

Unlike their primate relatives, humans developed the ability to take quick, deep inhalations followed by prolonged, controlled exhalations. This capability meant they could speak in phrases and sentences, extending the duration of their exhalations up to seven times longer than their resting exhalation. In contrast, nonhuman primates could only extend their exhalations to 2-3 times their resting duration. This advancement enabled humans to produce lengthy phrases without frequent pauses for breath.

## SPEECH THAT CHOKED

The journey toward sophisticated speech has inbuilt flaws in it. As humans began to speak, their vocal cords underwent dramatic transformations. The pharynx, the muscular tube that connects the nasal and oral cavities to the larynx, is narrowed and elongated compared to our short-necked ancestors. Additionally, the tongue moved posteriorly from the oral cavity to the pharynx. These changes, while facilitating speech, also introduced new challenges. Repositioning the tongue and elongating the pharynx increased the risk of pharyngeal collapse, a primary cause of obstructive sleep apnea.

The larynx works as a valve to shuttle food into the stomach and protect us from inhaling it and other objects. Like a gatekeeper, the larynx was positioned towards the top of the throat. As humans babbled, the larynx sank, opening up space in the back of the mouth and producing a more comprehensive range of vocalizations and volumes. Our lips grew smaller, thinner, and less bulbous, making it easier to manipulate. Tongues become flexible, making it easy to control sounds, slipping farther down the throat and pushing the jaws forward. Moreover, the dual-purpose path used for food and air and the extra space created at the back of the mouth heightened the risk of choking while eating and made breathing harder for us. We are the only animals that easily choke on food and die.

## JUT OUT JAWS

Our ancestors had prominent jaws that jutted out from their skulls, a feature known as prognathism. Their faces projected away from the neurocranium, giving them a strong, protruding appearance. Early hominins had large, powerful jaws that allowed them to chew tough plant material and raw meat. The pronounced prognathism allowed them to withstand the significant forces produced by strong biting and chewing. This was essential for survival, as their diet required robust mastication capabilities.

The erect man's spell over the fire was magical. He used it as he wished, cooking food that released enormous power and spending less time chewing. With more power, his brain developed, and with less work, his teeth diminished in size, reducing their prognathism.

Twelve thousand years ago, sapiens stopped gathering wild roots and vegetables and hunting games. They started growing their food. They transformed from hunters to farmers, causing widespread instances of crooked teeth and deformed mouths. Smaller teeth and jaws were sufficient for their softer, cooked foods.

Then, about 300 years ago, the worst happened: The Industrial Revolution of farmed foods. Within just a few generations of eating this processed stuff, modern humans became the worst breathers in the animal kingdom. It was severely damaging; it deteriorated our faces. Mouths shrank, and facial bones grew stunted. The incidence of crooked teeth and jaws increased. Our mouth was overcrowded with teeth.

Our ancestors chewed for hours a day, every day. They chewed so much that their mouths, teeth, throats, and faces grew broad, strong, and pronounced. Our foods are so soft that once hard-working teeth now have little job and are simply rotting. The only ones who benefited from this whole drama are dentists. The worst affected are breathing.

The small jaws altered the airway structure, making it more vertical and reducing the size of the nasal cavity. This change facilitated the development of speech. However, the narrower airway also introduced potential issues like sleep apnea and other breathing-related conditions.

Speech made us choke, collapse the airways mid-sleep, and snore like a devil. Despite these challenges, the benefits of speech far outweighed the risks. The ability to communicate complex ideas, share knowledge across generations, and form intricate social bonds propelled humanity forward. The fine control of breath, the evolution of the vocal tract, and the cognitive leaps all contributed to the rich and diverse languages we speak today. Speech is not an invention, but an evolution from the simple utterances of early hominins to the elaborate languages of modern humans.

No matter how upright we walk, how large the human brain grows, how much energy we lavish upon it, and how beautifully we sing, it's not these individual abilities but the combination of the above traits that make us indisputable. Our intelligence has always been so much bigger than our brain that it cannot be traced to a single organ, regardless of size. The truth is plain in hominin evolution: human brains are more advanced than respiratory systems, and our breaths were massively traded for the intelligence we pursue.

## MYSTERIOUS LUNGS

We have gone through the journey our ancestors went through in their lives, the pain, the happiness, and their hot breath, but what about the lungs, the master of the respiratory system? Unfortunately, lungs are made of spongy soft tissues that do not fossilize, so we have no idea what the journey of the hominin lungs was. The fact is the lungs of the modern great apes are structurally similar to humans, so we can deduce that the lungs of earlier homo species were not significantly different from our own.

Lung size varied according to body size. Neanderthals, for example, had 20% larger lung capacities than modern humans. The reason is apparent: they have larger and more powerful ribcages due to their larger body mass. They needed greater oxygen consumption to maintain the basic metabolism of a heavier body, larger brain, and muscles. Other than lungs, who can oxygenate their gigantic bodies, they, too, improved their size.

# CHAPTER 7

# FUTURE

*"If working apart, we're a force powerful enough to destabilize our planet, surely working together, we are powerful enough to save it."* -Sir David Attenborough

The best way to predict the future is to look back at the past and assume past trends will continue. Past showcased how we evolved, and with that vast knowledge, we can make educated guesses about what may happen in the future. Looking into our past paints a bleak future.

## 2.5 BILLION YEARS AGO

Earth was home to a single supercontinent called Pangaea, surrounded by a large ocean called Panthalassa. The vast landmass of Pangaea challenged life and presented extreme climatic conditions. The south shivered under ice caps, cold and arid, while the north sweated from the scorching sun.

Even though the situation seemed gloomy, life flourished by overcoming the challenges with innovations. Reptiles, with their super thick, moisture-retaining skin, deserted their amphibian kin and kiths and set for a brave voyage into the vast land of Pangaea. With some significant changes, they flourished and were well-positioned to take over the supercontinent. Meanwhile, bony fish dominated the Permian Sea.

Boom: A volcanic eruption in north Siberia killed 96 percent of all marine species and 70 percent of land animals. For 2 million years, Siberia spit lava continuously on the face of the earth, flooding 2.7 million square miles with blood-red magma. Although Siberia didn't drench the world with lava, it led to a domino effect that sanitized the entire earth. The eruption released enormous amounts of gasses dominated by carbon dioxide into the atmosphere.

The skies darkened with ash and gasses, generating acid rain. The relentless warming pushed the planet into an extreme greenhouse state, where temperatures soared to an incredible 100-104 Degrees Fahrenheit. The intense heat and the toxic atmosphere led to the collapse of ecosystems, making the hot spell intolerable for marine and terrestrial beings. Life struggled to survive. Seven out of ten land beings perished to death. Even plants were not spared.

The situation was more tragic in the water world. Ocean water becomes warmer and denser, creating an impenetrable barrier preventing oxygen from mixing into the deep ocean. Oceans absorbed large quantities of carbon dioxide and plummeted the pH of seawater, making it acidic. Beneath the ocean surface, the creatures that had once thrived started suffocating in the anoxic water, and they witnessed their skeletons being dissolved into the acidic water.

Lava rich in nutrients like phosphorus flowed copiously into the seawater. It benefited phytoplankton, including algae. With explosive growth, algae bloomed on the ocean's surface. They produced oxygen by photosynthesis. Waves and winds helped mix oxygen in the sea's uppermost layers. What about the deep sea? Below these precious layers, oxygen became a rare commodity. The matter worsened even more when these algae died. Their bodies sank to the bottom of the seabed, where they decomposed, consuming the leftover oxygen. This further depleted the oxygen, creating massive dead zones where life could no longer survive. The oceans, once vibrant with life, became barren and desolate. Around nine out of ten, organisms in the water were suffocated to death.

Within 15 million years, the catastrophic chain of events led to one of Earth's most severe mass extinctions, the Great Dying. It took double the time to recover from this catastrophe, 30 million years, for life to resurrect. New life forms filled the vacant niches left by the extinction.

## THE TIMES NOW

*"The end- permian rock record cannot currently provide the temporal and spatial resolution to make specific predictions about expected changes in the coming decades or centuries, but increasing evidence that*

> *the end-Permian mass extinction was precipitated by a rapid release of CO2 into earth's atmosphere is a valuable reminder that the best- and most sober- ing - analogs for our near future may lie deeper in earth's past."* - Payne and Clapham, 2012

You may have an idea of my point of view. Yes, it is easy to replace the carbon dioxide emission from the Siberian trap with industries and vehicles burning fossil fuels and releasing carbon dioxide. Not only burning fossil fuels, but clearing forests and relentless industrial expansion releases vast amounts of greenhouse gasses. We came to the world breathing carbon dioxide, but billions of years ago, we changed the gear to oxygen, which generously made us sizable. Now, we depend on it for our survival.

Unlike the slow geological timescale of the Siberian drama, which took millions of years to make the earth a toxic chamber, today's changes are happening in the blink of an eye. In just a few centuries, particularly the last few decades with the Industrial Revolution, the Earth's temperature has begun to rise at an alarming rate.

Let's examine some stats to analyze the rate at which we are nearing an upcoming catastrophe. The ocean absorbs 93% of atmospheric heat and 31% of atmospheric carbon dioxide, acting as a carbon sink. From the start of the Industrial Revolution, the pH of ocean waters has dropped from 8.21 to 8.10, leading to a 30% increase in acidity.

Atmospheric carbon dioxide is 50% higher than before the Industrial Revolution. The annual rate of increase in atmospheric carbon dioxide over the past 60 years is about 100 times faster than previous natural increases, such as those that occurred at the end of the last ice age 11,000-17,000 years ago. Before the Industrial Revolution started in the mid-1700s, atmospheric carbon dioxide was 280 ppm or less. But today, atmospheric carbon dioxide is more than 419 ppm, rapidly snowballing into a big disaster. The rate at which carbon dioxide gets infused into our atmosphere is unusual in the last 25 million years.

By adding more carbon dioxide to the atmosphere, we are supercharging the natural greenhouse effect, causing global temperature to rise. According to observations by the NOAA Global Monitoring Lab, in 2021, carbon dioxide alone was responsible for about two-thirds of the total heating influence of all human-produced greenhouse gases. The result is that air had become toxic, a silent killer that claimed lives with each breath. More than 32% of all mortalities were now linked to air pollution, a staggering figure highlighting the human cost of this environmental crisis.

The undeniable truth is that the oceans are getting warmer, ice caps are melting, and extreme weather events are becoming more frequent. The increasing acidity in the ocean is weakening the skeleton and protective hard shell armor of our marine buddies. Dead zones are appearing in the water world, giving a small space for the fish to survive. This helps our fishermen with excessive fishing and beefing the pocket. The changes are so rapid that the species are finding difficulty in adapting to their changing environment.

Our oceans are becoming nutritious as excess fertilizers wash out into the seawater. Algae blooms are already creating many problems, making our water bodies anoxic and leading to the death of aquatic life. The oxygen concentration in our ocean has decreased by two percent in just the last fifty years. Oxygen loves cold water, but as our oceans are getting warmer, it just doesn't get soluble.

If global energy demand continues to multiply and we decide to meet it mostly with fossil fuels, atmospheric carbon dioxide could be 800 ppm or higher by the end of this century—conditions not seen on Earth for nearly 50 million years.

A recent study in mice found that exposure to about 900 ppm carbon dioxide directly impacted lung function and structure. These elevated carbon dioxides altered the alveoli's physical structure of the mice. The catch is the most affected were infants' little lungs, especially those exposed to higher carbon dioxide levels throughout pregnancy and early life. The lungs of adult mice that were not exposed to elevated CO2 during early life did not show signs of impairment because adult lungs are fully grown. The fact that we should keep in mind is that mice are naturally able to better tolerate increases in carbon dioxide levels due to their burrowing habits. The troubling question is, what about us humans? The breath is going to affect our lungs for sure. What about our kidneys, skin, bones, brain, etc?

Howwever, a critical difference exists between the Siberian catastrophe and the current crisis. In the past, natural forces wrote about the world's fate. But today, humanity has both the power to destroy and the potential to save. The story of the Siberian Traps is a tale of nature's raw, uncontrollable force. Today's story is the result of human choices, the legacy of a civilization that harnessed the power of the Earth's resources without fully understanding the consequences.

The Earth's atmosphere, once so resilient, was now fragile. The rise in CO2 was a warning, a signal that time was running out. The world had a choice: to continue down a path that led to catastrophe or to take bold, decisive action to protect the planet for future generations. With this realization also came a ray of hope. The same ingenuity that had fueled the Industrial Revolution could now be turned toward solutions—toward renewable energy, sustainable practices, and preserving the delicate balance that can sustain life on Earth. The story of the Earth's atmosphere was still being written, and the next chapter depended on today's choices.

## 10000 YEARS LATER

My choice is later, as the world faces a new chapter in its history, humanity will heed the warnings of the ancient world and choose a different path if the story continues. Writing about the future is exciting, like writing a fantasy tale.

Although it's hard to predict the future, it's sure that the world will probably change in ways we can't imagine. In the distant future, the earth will be remembered as their ancestors' home, where the humans originated. Humans would have outgrown their earthy homes, occupying Mars and beyond the solar system. If so, they will initially depend on bulky suits in an artificial habitat with big oxygen-generating factories. Their alveoli will get larger and have a greater surface area, capable of extracting oxygen even from thin air. As an intermediate stage, we may develop bimodal breathing organs supporting our transition to the new environment.

With successful mutation and gene editing, the lungs will develop specialized cells capable of extracting energy from nitrogen, sulfur, carbon dioxide, carbon monoxide, methane, etc., reducing their dependence on oxygen. This is not new; our microbial ancestors were masters in these technologies, and some still do it. In our body, too, most of the bacteria in the large intestine still live in anaerobic conditions; our respiratory system may recruit them to assist us in breathing.

We may develop a symbiotic relationship with these microbes, embedding them in our lung cells and bloodstream, assisting in the breakdown of gasses and energy production. These symbiotic relationships can be exploited to extract energy directly from sunlight, like our plant buddies. If this happens, it will allow humans to generate power from multiple sources, reducing their dependence on food and oxygen. People could survive in environments once considered inhospitable, from the depths of the oceans to the extremes of the solar system.

Looking into human physiology, we will transfer to thoracic breathing, as it will be more than enough. Our diaphragms may get weaker. Our lungs will produce more mucus to fight pollutants and irritants. We will be more immune to diseases. Our brains will be smaller, giving some space for our faces to grow. As we shift to a soft diet, our jaws are shrinking and will further shrink. We will probably lose our wisdom teeth. We will live longer, taller, and less muscular. Globalization and sexual selection might make us more attractive and more uniform in appearance.

As a closing note, I urge us to breathe purposefully, knowing we evolve further with each breath. From the first whisper of carbon dioxide in primordial oceans to the magical power of oxygen, breath has been both the slayer and the driver of evolution. In this ongoing evolution of breath, humanity holds both the responsibility and the power to ensure that future generations can inhale the same air that has sustained life for billions of years. Will life be as resilient as this time? Acid-tolerant plants have evolved in the Black Triangle, where we've done so much to destroy an ecosystem. If life can survive the five mass extinctions, it can survive anything. Life will continue for sure. Will we humans survive? The answer lies in the breath we take. Breath is a story that evolved long before us and will continue long after us.

# REFERENCES


## ORIGIN OF LIFE

Abiogenesis. (2024, August 12). In Wikipedia.

Connor, A. N. (2020). Searching high and low for the origins of life. Knowable Magazine.

Cowing, K. (2024, March 16). Even Inactive Hydrothermal Smokers Are Densely Colonized By Microbial Communities - Astrobiology. Astrobiology.

Facts About Earth - NASA Science. (n.d.).

Gregory, T.R. The Evolution of Complex Organs. Evo Edu Outreach 1, 358–389 (2008).

Hartman H. Photosynthesis and the origin of life. Orig Life Evol Biosph. 1998 Oct; 28 (4-6):515-21. doi: 10.1023/a:1006 548904157. PMID: 11536891.

Introduction. (1999). Science and Creationism - NCBI Bookshelf.

Mheslinga. (2022, September 30). The origin of life on Earth, explained. University of Chicago News. .

National Academy of Sciences (US). Science and Creationism: A View from the National Academy of Sciences: Second Edition. Washington (DC): National Academies Press (US); 1999. Evidence Supporting Biological Evolution. Available from:

National Academy of Sciences (US). Science and Creationism: A View from the National Academy of Sciences: Second Edition. Washington (DC): National Academies Press (US); 1999. Human Evolution. Available from:

National Academy of Sciences (US). Science and Creationism: A View from the National Academy of Sciences: Second Edition. Washington (DC): National Academies Press (US); 1999. The Origin of the Universe, Earth, and Life. Available from:

NEO Basics. (n.d.). .

On the origin of biochemistry at an alkaline hydrothermal vent, William Martin And Michael J Russell

Page, M. L., & Lane, N. (2009b, October 13). How life evolved: 10 steps to the first cells. New Scientist.

Russell, M. J. (2018). Green Rust: The Simple Organizing 'Seed' of All Life? Life, 8(3), 35.

Sackville, Michael & Cameron, Christopher & Brauner, Colin. (2023). Gills are not used for gas exchange in the suspension-feeding hemichordate Protoglossus graveolens. 10.1101/2023.08.22.553704.

Sleep, N. H. (2010). The Hadean-Archaean Environment. Cold Spring Harbor Perspectives in Biology, 2(6).

Sun: Facts - NASA Science. (n.d.).

The origin of life: the submarine alkaline vent theory at 30 Julyan H. E. Cartwright And Michael J. Russell

Trevors, J. (2006). The Big Bang, Superstring Theory and the origin of life on the Earth. Theory in Biosciences, 124 (3-4), 403-412.

## CARBON DIOXIDE

Herschy, B., Whicher, A., Camprubi, E., Watson, C., Dartnell, L., Ward, J., G. Evans, J. R., & Lane, N. (2014). An Origin-of-Life Reactor to Simulate Alkaline Hydrothermal Vents. *Journal of Molecular Evolution*, *79*(5), 213-227.

Morse, J.W., Mackenzie, F.T. Hadean Ocean Carbonate Geochemistry. *Aquatic Geochemistry* 4, 301–319 (1998).

Mrnjavac, N., Wimmer, J. L. E., Brabender, M., Schwander, L., & Martin, W. (2023, October 19). The Moon-Forming Impact and the Autotrophic Origin of Life. ChemPlusChem.

Walker, J.C.G. Carbon dioxide on the early earth. Origins Life Evol Biosphere 16, 117–127 (1985).

White LM, Russell MJ, Mielke RE, Shibuya T, Christensen L, Bhartia R, Cable ML, Stockton A, Stucky GD, Kanik I. Alkaline hydrothermal vents: assembling the redox protein construction kit on icy worlds. 44th Lunar and Planetary Science Conference. 2013. Available at: . Accessed June 21, 2024.

Why do we have an ocean? (n.d.-b).

## NITROUS OXIDE

Bruce, D. F. (2008, October 28). Arginine: Heart Benefits and Side Effects. WebMD.

Eby, G. A. (2005). Strong humming for one hour daily to terminate chronic rhinosinusitis in four days: A case report and hypothesis for action by stimulation of endogenous nasal nitric oxide production. Medical Hypotheses, 66(4), 851-854.

Feelisch, M., & Martin, J. (1995). The early role of nitric oxide in evolution. Trends in ecology & evolution, 10 12, 496-9. .

J. (2001, November 6). Overactive Sympathetic Nervous System Archives - Dr. Nicholas L. DePace, M.D., F.A.C.C. Dr. Nicholas L. DePace, M.D., F.A.C.C.

Knuf K, Maani CV. Nitrous Oxide. [Updated 2023 Aug 28]. In: StatPearls [Internet]. Treasure Island (FL): StatPearls Publishing; 2024 Jan-. Available from:

Laughing Gas May Have Helped Warm Early Earth and Given Breath to Life. (2018, August 22). News Center.

Olson, K., Donald, J., Dombkowski, R., & Perry, S. (2012). Evolutionary and comparative aspects of nitric oxide, carbon monoxide and hydrogen sulfide. Respiratory Physiology & Neurobiology, 184, 117-129. .

Premont, R. T., Reynolds, J. D., Zhang, R., & Stamler, J. S. (2020, January 3). Role of Nitric Oxide Carried by Hemoglobin in Cardiovascular Physiology. Circulation Research.

Shepherd, M., Giordano, D., Verde, C., & Poole, R. K. (2022). The Evolution of Nitric Oxide Function: From Reactivity in the Prebiotic Earth to Examples of Biological Roles and Therapeutic Applications. Antioxidants, 11(7), 1222.

Stortenbeker, N., Wessels, H. J., Speth, D. R., & Kartal, B. (2023). Enrichment and characterization of a nitric oxide-reducing microbial community in a continuous bioreactor. Nature Microbiology, 8(8), 1574-1586.

Why deep oceans gave life to the first big, complex organisms. (2018, December 12). Stanford Doerr School of Sustainability.

## OXYGEN

Braakman, R., & Smith, E. (2012). The Emergence and Early Evolution of Biological Carbon-Fixation. PLoS Computational Biology, 8. .

Cardona, T., Murray, J. W., & Rutherford, A. W. (2015). Origin and Evolution of Water Oxidation before the Last Common

Ancestor of the Cyanobacteria. Molecular Biology and Evolution, 32(5), 1310-1328.

Dapcevich, M. (2021, December 8). Mass Extinction Event 2 Billion Years Ago Killed 99% of Life on Earth, Study Finds - EcoWatch. EcoWatch.

Fischer, Woodward W., James Hemp, and Jena E. Johnson. "Evolution of oxygenic photosynthesis." Annual Review of Earth and Planetary Sciences 44 (2016): 647-683.

Margulis, Lynn; Sagan, Dorion (1986). "Chapter 6, "The Oxygen Holocaust"". Microcosmos: Four Billion Years of Microbial Evolution. California: University of California Press. p. 99. ISBN 9780520210646.

Olson, J. M. (2006, February 2). Photosynthesis in the Archean Era. Photosynthesis Research (Print).

Rizvi, S., Raza, S. T., Ahmed, F., Ahmad, A., Abbas, S., & Mahdi, F. (2014). The Role of Vitamin E in Human Health and Some Diseases. Sultan Qaboos University Medical Journal, 14(2), e157.

Sessions, Alex L., David M. Doughty, Paula V. Welander, Roger E. Summons, and Dianne K. Newman. "The continuing puzzle of the great oxidation event." Current biology 19, no. 14 (2009): R567-R574.

Timmins GS, Jackson SK, Swartz HM. The evolution of bioluminescent oxygen consumption as an ancient oxygen detoxification mechanism. J Mol Evol. 2001; 52(4):321-332. doi:10.1007/s002 390010162

W. Hodgskiss, M. S., Crockford, P. W., Peng, Y., Wing, B. A., & Horner, T. J. (2019). A productivity collapse to end Earth's Great Oxidation. Proceedings of the National Academy of Sciences of the United States of America, 116(35), 17207-17212.

Ward, L. M., & Shih, P. M. (2021). Granick revisited: Synthesizing evolutionary and ecological evidence for the late origin of bacteriochlorophyll via ghost lineages and horizontal gene transfer. PLoS ONE, 16(1).

West, J. B. (2022). The strange history of atmospheric oxygen. Physiological Reports, 10(6).

## SYMBIOSIS

Azuma, Y., Tsuru, S., Habuchi, M. et al. Synthetic symbiosis between a cyanobacterium and a ciliate toward novel chloroplast-like endosymbiosis. Sci Rep 13, 6104 (2023).

Britannica, T. Editors of Encyclopaedia (2024, June 12). Paramecium. Encyclopedia Britannica.

Brunk, C. F., & Marshall, C. R. (2024). Opinion: The Key Steps in the Origin of Life to the Formation of the Eukaryotic Cell. Life, 14(2). https://doi.org/10.3390/life14020226

Cooper GM. The Cell: A Molecular Approach. 2nd edition. Sunderland (MA): Sinauer Associates; 2000. The Origin and Evolution of Cells. Available from:

Craig, J. M., Kumar, S., & Hedges, S. B. (2023). The origin of eukaryotes and rise in complexity were synchronous with the rise in oxygen. *Frontiers in Bioinformatics, 3.*

Gabaldón, T. (2021, October 8). Origin and Early Evolution of the Eukaryotic Cell. Annual Review of Microbiology.

Kelly RM, Adams MW. Metabolism in hyperthermophilic microorganisms. Antonie Van Leeuwenhoek. 1994; 66 (1-3):247-270. doi:10.1007/BF00871643

Martin, W. F., Garg, S., & Zimorski, V. (2015). Endosymbiotic theories for eukaryote origin. Philosophical Transactions of the Royal Society B: Biological Sciences, 370(1678).

Martin W, Müller M. The hydrogen hypothesis for the first eukaryote. Nature. 1998; 392(6671):37-41. doi:10.1038/32096

Mitchell, D. R. (2016). Evolution of Cilia. Cold Spring Harbor Perspectives in Biology, 9(1).

Sephus, CD., Fer, E., Garcia, A. K., Adam, Z. R., Schwieterman, E. W., & Kacar, B. (2022). Earliest Photic Zone Niches Probed by Ancestral Microbial Rhodopsins. Molecular Biology and Evolution, 39(5).

Zita Carvalho-Santos, Juliette Azimzadeh, José. B. Pereira-Leal, Mónica Bettencourt-Dias; Tracing the origins of centrioles, cilia, and flagella. J Cell Biol 25 July 2011; 194 (2): 165–175. doi:

# ORIGIN OF MULTICELLULAR ORGANISMS

Alberts B, Johnson A, Lewis J, et al. Molecular Biology of the Cell. 4th edition. New York: Garland Science; 2002. An Overview of Gene Control. Available from:

Cooper, G. M. (2000). The Origin and Evolution of Cells. The Cell - NCBI Bookshelf.

Droser, M. L., & Gehling, J. G. (2015). The advent of animals: The view from the Ediacaran. *Proceedings of the National Academy of Sciences, 112*(16), 4865-4870.

Droser, M. L., & Gehling, J. G. (2015). The advent of animals: The view from the Ediacaran. *Proceedings of the National Academy of Sciences of the United States of America, 112*(16), 4865-4870.

*Evidence of the world's oldest meal may have been discovered.* (2022, November 24). Natural History Museum. .

*First Animals.* (n.d.). Oxford University Museum of Natural History. .

Grüber, G., Manimekalai, M. S. S., Mayer, F., & Müller, V. (2014). ATP synthases from archaea: The beauty of a molecular motor. Biochimica et Biophysica Acta (BBA) - Bioenergetics, 1837(6), 940-952.

Gumsley, A., Manby, G., Domańska-Siuda, J., Nejbert, K., & Michalski, K. (2020). Caught between two continents: First identification of the Ediacaran Central Iapetus Magmatic Province in

Western Svalbard with palaeogeographic implications during final Rodinia breakup. *Precambrian Research*, *341*, 105622.

Herron, M. D., Hackett, J. D., Aylward, F. O., & Michod, R. E. (2009). Triassic origin and early radiation of multicellular volvocine algae. Proceedings of the National Academy of Sciences, 106(9), 3254-3258.

Ocean, S. (2023, May 11). *Jellyfish and Comb Jellies*. Smithsonian Ocean. .

Pehr, K., Love, G. D., Kuznetsov, A., Podkovyrov, V., Junium, C. K., Shumlyanskyy, L., Sokur, T., & Bekker, A. (2018). Ediacara biota flourished in oligotrophic and bacterially dominated marine environments across Baltica. *Nature Communications*, *9*.

Pehr, K., Love, G. D., Kuznetsov, A., Podkovyrov, V., Junium, C. K., Shumlyanskyy, L., Sokur, T., & Bekker, A. (2018). Ediacara biota flourished in oligotrophic and bacterially dominated marine environments across Baltica. *Nature Communications*, *9*(1), 1-10.

Reynolds, A. (2008). Ernst Haeckel and the Theory of the Cell State: Remarks on the History of a Bio-Political Metaphor. History of Science.

Ros-Rocher, N., Pérez-Posada, A., Leger, M. M., & Ruiz-Trillo, I. (2021). The origin of animals: An ancestral reconstruction of the unicellular-to-multicellular transition. *Open Biology*, *11*(2).

Schirrmeister, B. E., Antonelli, A., & Bagheri, H. C. (2011). The origin of multicellularity in cyanobacteria. BMC Evolutionary Biology, 11, 45.

Schultz, D. T., Haddock, S. H., Bredeson, J. V., Green, R. E., Simakov, O., & Rokhsar, D. S. (2023). Ancient gene linkages support ctenophores as sister to other animals. *Nature, 618*(7963), 110-117.

Sender, R., Fuchs, S., & Milo, R. (2016). Revised Estimates for the Number of Human and Bacteria Cells in the Body. PLoS Biology, 14(8).

The momentous transition to multicellular life may not have been so hard after all. (2024, March 22). Science | AAAS.

V. (n.d.). *Chapter 2–The Breath of Life in Insects and Humans.* Pressbooks.

Williams, J.J., Mills, B.J.W. & Lenton, T.M. A tectonically driven Ediacaran oxygenation event. Nat Commun 10, 2690 (2019).

Www.Ediacaran.org. (n.d.). www. Ediacaran. org.

## AQUATIC BREATHING

Bakshani, C. R., L, A., Althaus, M., Wilcox, M. D., Pearson, J. P., Bythell, J. C., & Burgess, J. G. (2018). Evolutionary conservation of the antimicrobial function of mucus: A first defence against infection. *Npj Biofilms and Microbiomes, 4*(1), 1-12.

Frisdal, A., & Trainor, P. A. (2014). Development and Evolution of the Pharyngeal Apparatus. *Wiley Interdisciplinary Reviews. Developmental Biology, 3*(6), 403.

Ghiselin, M. T. (2024, February 9). cephalochordate. Encyclopedia Britannica.

Gillis, J. A., Fritzenwanker, J. H., & Lowe, C. J. (2011). A stem-deuterostome origin of the vertebrate pharyngeal transcriptional network. *Proceedings of the Royal Society B: Biological Sciences, 279*(1727), 237-246.

GONZALEZ, P., & CAMERON, C. B. (2009). The gill slits and pre-oral ciliary organ of Protoglossus (Hemichordata: Enteropneusta) are filter-feeding structures. *Biological Journal of the Linnean Society, 98*(4), 898-906.

Graham, A., & Richardson, J. (2012). Developmental and evolutionary origins of the pharyngeal apparatus. *EvoDevo, 3*, 24.

He, T., Zhu, M., Mills, J. W., Wynn, P. M., Zhuravlev, A. Y., Tostevin, R., Yang, A., Poulton, S. W., & Shields, G. A. (2019). Possible links between extreme oxygen perturbations and the Cambrian radiation of animals. *Nature Geoscience, 12*(6), 468.

Hubot, N., Giering, S. L., & Lucas, C. H. (2022). Similarities between the biochemical composition of jellyfish body and mucus. *Journal of Plankton Research, 44*(2), 337-344.

Huizen, J. (2023, December 20). Mucus: Where does it come from and how is it formed?

L. (2021, February 28). *22.3: Different Types of Respiratory Systems*. Biology LibreTexts.

Releasing our inner jellyfish. (2018, August 16). Press Office.

Saltzman, M. R., Young, S. A., Kump, L. R., Gill, B. C., Lyons, T. W., & Runnegar, B. (2011). Pulse of atmospheric oxygen during the late Cambrian. *Proceedings of the National Academy of Sciences, 108*(10), 3876-3881.

# MORPHOLOGICAL FEATURES OF GAS EXCHANGERS

Maina, J. (2002). Structure, function and evolution of the gas exchangers: Comparative perspectives. Journal of Anatomy, 201(4), 281-304.

FISH

Acid-Base Balance | Anatomy and Physiology II. (n.d.). .

At Home in the Water, "Condemned" to Life on Land. (2021, October 13). Water Blogged.

Bainton CR, Kirkwood PA, Sears TA. On the transmission of the stimulating effects of carbon dioxide to the muscles of respiration. J Physiol. 1978; 280:249-272.

Baker, D. W., Sardella, B., Rummer, J. L., Sackville, M., & Brauner, C. J. (2015). Hagfish: Champions of CO2 tolerance question the origins of vertebrate gill function. *Scientific Reports, 5*.

Colin M Cleary, Thiago S Moreira, Ana C Takakura, Mark T Nelson, Thomas A Longden, Daniel K Mulkey (2020) Vascular control of the CO2/H+-dependent drive to breathe eLife 9: e59499

Deeper origin of gill evolution suggested "active lifestyle" link in. (2017, February 9). The University of Cambridge. https://www.cam.ac.uk/research/news/deeper-origin-of-gill-evolution-suggests-active-lifestyle-link-in-early-vertebrates

Gillis JA, Tidswell OR. The Origin of Vertebrate Gills. Curr Biol. 2017; 27(5):729-732. doi:10.1016/j. cub.2017.01.022

Graham, A., Richardson, J. Developmental and evolutionary origins of the pharyngeal apparatus. EvoDevo 3, 24 (2012). https://doi.org/10.1186/2041-9139-3-24

Hou J-B, Hughes NC, Hopkins MJ, Shu D. 2023 Gill function in an early arthropod and the widespread adoption of the countercurrent exchange mechanism. R. SoC. Open Sci. 10: 230341. https://doi.org/10.1098/rsos.230341

Junho Eom, Henrik Lauridsen, Chris M. Wood; Breathing versus feeding in the Pacific hagfish. J Exp Biol 15 March 2022; 225 (6): jeb243989. doi:

Pelster, B., & Bagatto, B. (2009). Respiration. Fish Physiology, 29, 289-309.

Sean T. Brennan, Tim K. Lowenstein, Juske Horita; Seawater chemistry and the advent of biocalcification. Geology 2004; ; 32 (6): 473–476. doi:

SMITH, G. E. (1930). Studies on the Structure and Development of Vertebrates. Nature, 126(3175), 341-343.

# TERRESTRIAL BREATHING

A., M., Hsieh, S. T., Gibb, A. C., & Blob, R. W. (2013). Vertebrate Land Invasions–Past, Present, and Future: An Introduction to the Symposium. Integrative and Comparative Biology, 53(2), 192-196.

Boodman, E. (2023, July 31). How an inconspicuous slaughterhouse keeps the world's premature babies alive. STAT.

Cupello, C., Hirasawa, T., Tatsumi, N., Yabumoto, Y., Gueriau, P., Isogai, S., Matsumoto, R., Saruwatari, T., King, A., Hoshino, M., Uesugi, K., Okabe, M., & Brito, P. M. (2022). Lung evolution in vertebrates and the water-to-land transition. ELife, 11.

Daniels, C. B., & Orgeig, S. (2003). Pulmonary Surfactant: The Key to the Evolution of Air Breathing. Physiology.

Daniels, C. B., Orgeig, S., Sullivan, L. C., Ling, N., Bennett, M. B., Schürch, S., Val, A. L., & Brauner, C. J. (2004). The Origin and Evolution of the Surfactant System in Fish: Insights into the Evolution of Lungs and Swim Bladders on JSTOR. Physiological and Biochemical Zoology: Ecological and Evolutionary Approaches, 732.

Daniels, C. B., Wood, P. G., Lopatko, O. V., Codd, J. R., Johnston, S. D., & Orgeig, S. (1999). Surfactant in the Gas Mantle of the Snail Helix aspersa. Physiological and Biochemical Zoology: Ecological and Evolutionary Approaches, 72(6), 691–698.

Das B. K. and MacBride Ernest William 1934The habits and structure of pseudapocryptes lanceolatus, a fish in the first stages of structural adaptation to aerial respirationProc. R. SoC. Lond. B.115422–430

Evolution of tetrapods. (2024, February 28). In Wikipedia.

Jew, C. J., Wegner, N. C., Yanagitsuru, Y., Tresguerres, M., & Graham, J. B. (2013). Atmospheric Oxygen Levels Affect Mudskipper Terrestrial Performance: Implications for Early Tetrapods. Integrative and Comparative Biology, 53(2), 248-257.

Orgeig, S., Morrison, J. L., & Daniels, C. B. (2011). Prenatal development of the pulmonary surfactant system and the influence of hypoxia. Respiratory Physiology & Neurobiology, 178(1), 129-145.

University of Alaska Fairbanks. (2012, October 16). Scientists identify likely origins of vertebrate air breathing. ScienceDaily. Retrieved April 10, 2024 from

We're more like primitive fishes than once believed. (2021, February 4). https://news.ku.dk/all_news/2021/02/were-more-like-primitive-fishes-than-once-believed/

## AMPHIBIANS

Adler, J. (2014, May 13). Did the Evolution of Animal Intelligence Begin With Tiktaalik? Smithsonian Magazine.

Anderson, Jason S.. "Tiktaalik". *The Canadian Encyclopedia*, 06 February 2024, *Historica Canada*. www.thecanadianencyclopedia.ca/en/article/tiktaalik. Accessed 18 May 2024.

Berner R.A., Canfield DE. A new model for atmospheric oxygen over Phanerozoic time. Am J Sci. 1989; 289(4):333-361. doi:10.2475/ajs.289.4.333

Bi, Xupeng et al. "Tracing the genetic footprints of vertebrate landing in non-teleost ray-finned fishes." Cell vol. 184,5 (2021): 1377-1391. e14. doi:10.1016/j. cell.2021.01.046

Carvalho, Olga & Gonçalves, Carlos. (2011). Comparative Physiology of the Respiratory System in the Animal Kingdom. The Open Biology Journal. 4. 10.2174/1874196701104010035.

Clement, A. M., & Long, J. A. (2010). Air-breathing adaptation in a marine Devonian lungfish. Biology Letters, 6(4), 509-512. https://doi.org/10.1098/rsbl.2009.1033

Darwin, Charles (1859) Page 190, reprinted 1872 by D. Appleton.

Dr. Biology. (2016, July 25). How did ancient fish make the evolutionary jump from gills to lungs?. ASU - Ask A Biologist. Retrieved May 15, 2024 from

Dunn, C. W. (2013). Evolution: Out of the Ocean. Current Biology, 23(6), R241-R243.

Farmer, CG. (1999). Evolution of the vertebrate cardio-pulmonary system: new insights. Annual review of physiology. 61. 573-92. 10.1146/annurev. physiol.61.1.573

Fossil find fills evolutionary gap between fish and land animals. (n.d.).

George, D., & Blieck, A. (2011). Rise of the Earliest Tetrapods: An Early Devonian Origin from Marine Environment. *PLoS ONE, 6*(7).

Graham, J. B., Aguilar, N. M., Dudley, R., & Gans, C. (1995). Implications of the late Palaeozoic oxygen pulse for physiology and evolution. Nature, 375(6527), 117-120.

Graham, Jeffrey B. "An evolutionary perspective for bimodal respiration: a biological synthesis of fish air breathing." American Zoologist 34.2 (1994): 229-237.

Graham R. Scott; Early insights into the evolution of respiratory and cardiovascular physiology in vertebrates. *J Exp Biol* 1 September 2015; 218 (18): 2818–2820. doi:

Hoffman, M., Taylor, B. E., & Harris, M. B. (2016). Evolution of lung breathing from a lungless primitive vertebrate. *Respiratory Physiology & Neurobiology, 224*, 11.

Lemberg, J. B., Daeschler, E. B., & Shubin, N. H. (2021). The feeding system of Tiktaalik roseae: An intermediate between suction feeding and biting. *Proceedings of the National Academy of Sciences of the United States of America, 118*(7). https://doi.org/10.1073/pnas.2016421118

Mutolo, D., Bongianni, F., Pantaleo, T., & Cinelli, E. (2021). The lamprey respiratory network: Some evolutionary aspects. *Respiratory Physiology & Neurobiology, 294*, 103766.

Stamati, K., Mudera, V., & Cheema, U. (2011). Evolution of oxygen utilization in multicellular organisms and implications for cell signaling in tissue engineering. *Journal of Tissue Engineering, 2*(1).

University of Alaska Fairbanks. "Scientists identify likely origins of vertebrate air breathing." ScienceDaily. ScienceDaily, 16 October 2012.

W. Hsia, C. C., Schmitz, A., Lambertz, M., Perry, S. F., & Maina, J. N. (2013). Evolution of Air Breathing: Oxygen Homeostasis and the Transitions from water to land and Sky. *Comprehensive Physiology, 3*(2), 849.

## REPTILES

Brainerd, E. L., & Owerkowicz, T. (2006). Functional morphology and evolution of aspiration breathing in tetrapods. Respiratory Physiology & Neurobiology, 154 (1-2), 73-88.

Brainerd, E.L. New perspectives on the evolution of lung ventilation mechanisms in vertebrates. EBO 4, 1–28 (1999).

Cieri, R. L., Hatch, S. T., Capano, J. G., & Brainerd, E. L. (2020). Locomotor rib kinematics in two species of lizards and a new hypothesis for the evolution of aspiration breathing in amniotes. *Scientific Reports*, *10*(1), 1-10.

Communications. (2024, June 11). A Brief History of Mammals Part 1: The Early Synapsids. Philip J. Currie Dinosaur Museum.

Eme J, Klein W, Gadek A, et al. New insights into the early evolution of the amniote diaphragm. Zool Lett. 2020; 6:7. doi:10.1186/s40851-020-00160-5

Fogarty, M. J., & Sieck, G. C. (2019). Evolution and Functional Differentiation of the Diaphragm Muscle of Mammals. Comprehensive Physiology, 9(2), 715.

Hirasawa, T., & Kuratani, S. (2013). A new scenario of the evolutionary derivation of the mammalian diaphragm from shoulder muscles. Journal of Anatomy, 222(5), 504-517.

https://doi.org/10.1002/cphy.c180012

Lalremsanga, H.T.. (2021). Origin and Evolution of Reptiles.

Lambertz, M., Grommes, K., Kohlsdorf, T., & Perry, S. F. (2014). Lungs of the first amniotes: Why simple if they can be complex? *Biology Letters*, *11*(1).

Lambertz, M., Shelton, CD., Spindler, F., & Perry, S. F. (2016). A caseian point for the evolution of a diaphragm homologue among the earliest synapsids. *Annals of the New York Academy of Sciences*, *1385*(1), 3-20.

Merrell, A. J., & Kardon, G. (2013). Development of the diaphragm, a skeletal muscle essential for mammalian respiration. The FEBS Journal, 280(17).

Mosley, M. (2011, May 5). Anatomical clues to human evolution from fish. BBC News.

Origin of Reptiles | Zoology for IAS, IFoS and other competitive exams. (2017, July 3). IASZoology.com | Zoology and Entomology Articles - the Indian Administrative Service Zoology.

Perry SF, Similowski T, Klein W, Codd JR. The evolutionary origin of the mammalian diaphragm. *Respir Physiol Neurobiol*. 2010; 171(1):1-16. https://doi:10.1016/j.resp.2010.01.004

Ribs evolved for movement first, then co-opted for breathing - @theU. (2020, May 19).

The University of Chicago Magazine. (n.d.).

The University of Bonn. "Diaphragm, much older than expected." ScienceDaily. www.sciencedaily.com/releases/2016/11/1611181 03611.htm (accessed July 17, 2024).

W. Hsia, C. C., Schmitz, A., Lambertz, M., Perry, S. F., & Maina, J. N. (2013). Evolution of Air Breathing: Oxygen Homeostasis and the Transitions from water to land and sky. *Comprehensive Physiology, 3*(2), 849.

Wallden M. The diaphragm - More than an inspired design. J Bodyw Mov Ther. 2017; 21(3):342-349. doi:10.1016/j. jbmt .2016.11.015.

## BIRDS

Asher, H. (2024, March 8). How Birds Breathe Differently from Humans — An Darach Forest Therapy. An Darach Forest Therapy. .

How birds got their wings. (n.d.). Channels.

Peacock, A. J. (1998). ABC of oxygen: Oxygen at high altitude. BMJ: British Medical Journal, 317(7165), 1063-1066.

Scott GR. Elevated performance: the unique physiology of birds that fly at high altitudes. J Exp Biol. 2011 Aug 1; 214 (Pt 15):2455-62. doi: 10.1242/jeb.052548. PMID: 21753038.

The origin of birds. (n.d.).

## MAMMALS

Brusatte, S. (2024, February 20). How Mammals Conquered the World after the Asteroid Apocalypse. Scientific American.

Cabreira, S. F., Schultz, C. L., Puricelli Lora, L. H., Pakulski, C., Soares, M. B., Smith, M. M., & Richter, M. (2022). Diphyodont tooth replacement of Brasilodon—A Late Triassic eucynodont that challenges the time of origin of mammals. Journal of Anatomy, 241(6), 1424-1440.

Chiarenza, A. A., Farnsworth, A., Mannion, P. D., Lunt, D. J., Valdes, P. J., Morgan, J. V., & Allison, P. A. (2020). Asteroid impact, not volcanism, caused the end-Cretaceous dinosaur extinction. Proceedings of the National Academy of Sciences of the United States of America, 117(29), 17084-17093.

Deep Impact and the Mass Extinction of Species 65 Million Years Ago - NASA Science. (n.d.).

Geggel, L., & LiveScience. (2024, February 20). Meet the Ancient Reptile that Gave Rise to Mammals. Scientific American.

Gore, R. (n.d.). The Rise of Mammals. Science.

Hsia, C. W., Hyde, D. M., & Weibel, E. R. (2016). Lung Structure and the Intrinsic Challenges of Gas Exchange. Comprehensive Physiology, 6(2), 827.

https://www.earth.com/news/mammals-and-birds-became-warm-blooded-after-surviving-a-mass-extinction/

Humans are mammals. (n.d.). The Australian Museum.

Hunter, P. (2020). The rise of the mammals: Fossil discoveries combined with dating advances give insight into the great mammal expansion. EMBO Reports, 21(11).

Martinelli, A. G., Soares, M. B., & Schwanke, C. (2016). Two New Cynodonts (Therapsida) from the Middle-Early Late Triassic of Brazil and Comments on South American Probainognathians. PLOS ONE, 11(10), e0162945.

Morrison, R. (2023, January 9). In the Eye of Evolution: Why are Mammals Warm-Blooded? - Londolozi Blog. Blog.

Novacek, M. J. (1997). Mammalian evolution: An early record bristling with evidence. Current Biology, 7(8), R489-R491.

Ochs M, Nyengaard JR, Jung A, et al. The number of alveoli in the human lung. Am J Respir Crit Care Med. 2004; 169(1):120-124. doi:10.1164/rccm.200308-1107OC

Oskin, B. (2013, December 12). Earth's Greatest Killer Finally Caught. livescience.com.

Thecodont. (n.d.).

Torday, J. S., Rehan, V. K., Hicks, J. W., Wang, T., Maina, J., Weibel, E. R., Hsia, C. C., Sommer, R. J., & Perry, S. F. (2007). Deconvoluting lung evolution: From phenotypes to gene regulatory networks. Integrative and Comparative Biology, 47(4), 601-609.


## HUMAN BREATH


Balzeau, A., Albessard-Ball, L., Kubicka, A. M., Filippo, A., Beaudet, A., Santos, E., Bienvenu, T., Arsuaga, L., Bartsiokas, A., Berger, L., Brunet, M., Carlson, K. J., Daura, J., Gorgoulis, V. G., Grine, F. E., Harvati, K., Hawks, J., Herries, A., Hublin, J.,...

Buck, L. T. (2022). Frontal sinuses and human evolution. Science Advances.

Bastir M, García-Martínez D, Torres-Tamayo N, et al. Rib cage anatomy in Homo erectus suggests a recent evolutionary origin of modern human body shape. Nat Ecol Evol. 2020; 4(9):1178-1187. doi:10.1038/s41559-020-1240-4

Bastir M, Sanz-Prieto D, López-Rey JM, et al. The evolution, form and function of the human respiratory system. *J Anthropol Sci*. 2022; 100:141-172. https://doi:10.4436/JASS.10014

Bohannon, C. (2023). Eve. Hutchinson.

Burton, G. J., Moffett, A., & Keverne, B. (2015). Human evolution: Brain, birthweight and the immune system. Philosophical Transactions of the Royal Society B: Biological Sciences, 370(1663).

Campbell, R. M., Vinas, G., & Henneberg, M. (2022). Relationships between the hard and soft dimensions of the nose in Pan troglodytes and Homo sapiens reveal the positions of the nasal tips of Plio-Pleistocene hominids. PLoS ONE, 17(2).

Carotenuto F, Tsikaridze N, Rook L, et al. Venturing out safely: The biogeography of Homo erectus dispersal out of Africa. *J Hum Evol*. 2016; 95:1-12. https://doi:10.1016/j.jhevol.2016.02.005

Carotenuto F, Tsikaridze N, Rook L, et al. Venturing out safely: The biogeography of Homo erectus dispersal out of Africa. *J Hum Evol*. 2016; 95:1-12. https://doi:10.1016/j.jhevol.2016.02.005

De Boer, B. Evolution of speech and evolution of language. Psychon Bull Rev 24, 158–162 (2017).

Dunsworth, HM Origin of the Genus *Homo*. *Evo Edu Outreach* 3, 353–366 (2010).

Emes, Y., Aybar, B., & Yalçın, S. (2011). On The Evolution of Human Jaws and Teeth: A Review.

Frémondière, P., Thollon, L., Marchal, F., Fornai, C., Webb, N. M., & Haeusler, M. (2022). Dynamic finite-element simulations reveal the early origin of complex human birth pattern. Communications Biology, 5(1), 1-10.

Futrell, R. (n.d.). When was talking invented? A language scientist explains how this unique feature of human beings may have evolved. The Conversation.

García-Martínez, D., Torres-Tamayo, N., Torres-Sánchez, I., García-Río, F., Rosas, A., & Bastir, M. (2018). Ribcage measurements indicate greater lung capacity in Neanderthals and Lower Pleistocene hominins compared to modern humans. *Communications Biology, 1*.

Gea J. La especie humana: un largo camino para el sistema respiratorio [The evolution of the human species: a long journey for the respiratory system]. *Arch Bronconeumol*. 2008; 44(5):263-270.

GIDAY WOLDEGABRIEL, JAMES L. ARONSON, ROBERT C. WALTER; Geology, geochronology, and rift basin development in the central sector of the Main Ethiopia Rift. GSA Bulletin 1990; ; 102 (4): 439–458. doi: <0439:GGARBD>2.3.CO;2

Handwerk, B. (2022, August 24). Seven Million Years Ago, the Oldest Known Early Human Was Already Walking. Smithsonian Magazine. .

Harari, Y. N. (2015). Sapiens. Vintage Books.

How did humans evolve from apes? (n.d.). New Scientist. https://www.newscientist.com/question/humans-evolve-apes/

How Humans Evolved Supersize Brains | Quanta Magazine. (2022, September 29). Quanta Magazine.

Lieberman, Philip and McCarthy, Robert. "Tracking the Evolution of Language and Speech." Expedition Magazine 49, no. 2 (July, 2007): -. Accessed August 10, 2024.

Lovejoy CO. The origin of man. Science. 1981; 211(4480):341-350. doi:10.1126/science.211.4480.341

Lucia F. Jacobs, Basil el Jundi, Almut Kelber, Barbara Webb; The navigational nose: a new hypothesis for the function of the human external pyramid. *J Exp Biol* 6 February 2019; 222 (Suppl_1): jeb186924. doi:

M. F. Hammer, A. E. Woerner, F. L. Mendez, J. C. Watkins, J. D. Wall. Genetic evidence for archaic admixture in Africa. Proceedings of the National Academy of Sciences, 2011; DOI: 10.1073/pnas.1109300108.

MacLarnon AM, Hewitt GP. The evolution of human speech: the role of enhanced breathing control. Am J Phys Anthropol. 1999;

109(3):341-363. doi:https://10.1002/ (SICI) 1096-8644(199907)
109:3<341:: AID-AJPA5>3.0. CO; 2-2

Mladina, R., Skitarelić, N., & Vuković, K. (2009). Why do humans have such a prominent nose? The final result of phylogenesis: A significant reduction of the splanchocranium on account of the neurocranium. *Medical Hypotheses, 73*(3), 280-283.

Mladina R, Skitarelić N, Vuković K. Why do humans have such a prominent nose? The final result of phylogenesis: a significant reduction of the splanchocranium on account of the neurocranium. *Med Hypotheses.* 2009; 73(3):280-283. doi:10.1016/j. mehy.2009 .03.045

Mladina R, Skitarelić N, Vuković K. Why do humans have such a prominent nose? The final result of phylogenesis: a significant reduction of the splanchocranium on account of the neurocranium. Med Hypotheses. 2009; 73(3):280-283. https://doi:10.1016/j.m ehy.2009.03.045

Naftali S, Rosenfeld M, Wolf M, Elad D. The air-conditioning capacity of the human nose. Ann Biomed Eng. 2005; 33(4):545-553. https://doi:10.1007/s10439-005-2513-4

Nestor, J. (2021). Breath.

Niemitz, C. (2010). The evolution of the upright posture and gait—A review and a new synthesis. Die Naturwissenschaften, 97(3), 241-263.

Norman, B. (2014). Facial prognathism in the hominid and human species. *Soton.*

Padian, K. Evolution: Doing the locomotion. Nature 530, 416–417 (2016).

Reporter, G. S. (2023, November 20). Where did they all go? How Homo sapiens became the last human species left. The Guardian.

Rodman, P.S., & McHenry, H. M. (1979). Bioenergetics and the origin of hominid bipedalism. American Journal of Physical Anthropology, 52(1), 103-106.

Rosas, A., & Bastir, M. (2018). Ribcage measurements indicate greater lung capacity in Neanderthals and Lower Pleistocene hominins compared to modern humans. *Communications Biology*, *1*(1), 1-9.

Sarmiento, E. E. (2010). Comment on the Paleobiology and Classification of Ardipithecus ramidus. Science.

Sinuses offer a new way of studying the evolution of ancient humans. (2022, October 21). Natural History Museum.

Sinuses shed light on how humans got their unique skull shape. (2022, October 21).

Sockol, M. D., Raichlen, D. A., & Pontzer, H. (2007). Chimpanzee locomotor energetics and the origin of human bipedalism. Proceedings of the National Academy of Sciences, 104(30), 12265-12269.

Stansfield, E., Fischer, B., Grunstra, N.D.S. et al. The evolution of pelvic canal shape and rotational birth in humans. BMC Biol 19, 224 (2021).

Stickford, A.S.L., Stickford, J.L. Ventilation and Locomotion in Humans: Mechanisms, Implications, and Perturbations to the Coupling of These Two Rhythms. Springer Science Reviews 2, 95–118 (2014).

Suzana Herculano-Houzel, Jon H. Kaas; Gorilla and Orangutan Brains Conform to the Primate Cellular Scaling Rules: Implications for Human Evolution. Brain Behav Evol 1 February 2011; 77 (1): 33–44.

Takahashi R. The formation of the human paranasal sinuses. Acta Otolaryngol Suppl. 1984; 408:1-28. doi:10.3109/00016 488409121162

The University of Arizona. (2011, September 6). Ancient humans were mixing it up: Anatomically modern humans interbred with more archaic hominin forms while in Africa. ScienceDaily. Retrieved August 4, 2024 from www.sciencedaily. com/releases/2011/09/110905160918.htm.

The University of Zurich. (2022, May 10). Complex human childbirth and cognitive abilities are a result of walking upright. ScienceDaily. Retrieved August 8, 2024 from

Wayman, E. (2023, November 1). Becoming Human: The Evolution of Walking Upright. Smithsonian Magazine.

Wayman, E. (2023b, November 8). How Africa Became the Cradle of Humankind. Smithsonian Magazine.

Wu Y, Chen K, Ye Y, Zhang T, Zhou W. Humans navigate with stereo olfaction. *Proc Natl Acad Sci U S A*. 2020; 117(27):16065-16071. https://doi:10.1073/pnas.2004642117

Zaidi, A. A., Mattern, B. C., Claes, P., McEcoy, B., Hughes, C., & Shriver, M. D. (2017). Investigating the case of human nose shape and climate adaptation. *PLoS Genetics*, *13*(3).

## FUTURE

Burger, B. J., Vargas Estrada, M., & Gustin, M. S. (2019). What caused Earth's largest mass extinction event? New evidence from the Permian-Triassic boundary in northeastern Utah. Global and Planetary Change, 177, 81-100.

Climate Change: Atmospheric Carbon Dioxide. (2024, April 9). NOAA Climate.gov.

D'Amato, G., Cecchi, L., D'Amato, M., & Annesi-Maesano, I. (2014). Climate change and respiratory diseases. European Respiratory Review, 23(132), 161–169.

Gold, D. A., & Vermeij, G. J. (2023). Deep resilience: An evolutionary perspective on calcification in an age of ocean acidification. *Frontiers in Physiology, 14*.

Hoffman, H. J. (n.d.). The Permian extinction—when life nearly came to an end. Science.

Larcombe, A. N., Papini, M. G., Chivers, E. K., Berry, L. J., Lucas, R. M., & Wyrwoll, C. S. (2021). Mouse Lung Structure and

Function after Long-Term Exposure to an Atmospheric Carbon Dioxide Level Predicted by Climate Change Modeling. Environmental Health Perspectives, 129(1).

Longrich, N. R. (2022, March 18). Future evolution: from looks to brains and personality, how will humans change in the next 10,000 years? Big Think.

Permian Period. (2017, January 24). Science.

Quantifying the Ocean Carbon Sink. (2024, July 18). National Centers for Environmental Information (NCEI). .

Saito, R., Wörmer, L., Taubner, H., Kaiho, K., Takahashi, S., Tian, L., Ikeda, M., Summons, R. E., & Hinrichs, K. (2023). Centennial scale sequences of environmental deterioration preceded the end-Permian mass extinction. Nature Communications, 14(1), 1-8.

Sean T. Brennan, Tim K. Lowenstein, Juske Horita; Seawater chemistry and the advent of biocalcification. Geology 2004;; 32 (6): 473–476. doi:

Sperling, E. A., Boag, T. H., Duncan, M. I., Endriga, C. R., Marquez, J. A., Mills, D. B., Monarrez, P. M., Sclafani, J. A., Stockey, R. G., & Payne, J. L. (2022). Breathless through Time: Oxygen and Animals across Earth's History. The Biological Bulletin.

The Effects: Dead Zones and Harmful Algal Blooms | US EPA. (2024, January 3). US EPA. .

The Great Dying - NASA Science. (n.d.).

Tran, H. M., Tsai, F., Lee, Y., Chang, J., Chang, L., Chang, T., Chung, K. F., Kuo, H., Lee, K., Chuang, K., & Chuang, H. (2023). The impact of air pollution on respiratory diseases in an era of climate change: A review of the current evidence. Science of The Total Environment, 898, 166340.

VIDEO: Biological Impacts of Oxygen Loss in the Ocean: The Blinding Truth. (n.d.-b). UCSD-TV - University of California Television, San Diego.

World-first study shows increased atmospheric CO2 levels damage young lungs. (n.d.).

# MAY I ASK YOU FOR A SMALL FAVOR?

I want to express my sincere gratitude for choosing to invest your time in reading this book. Your decision to explore this work among countless others means a lot to me.

I hope that within these pages, you've discovered actionable insights that can enhance your daily life. Your journey doesn't have to end here, though.

**May I kindly request an additional 30 seconds of your valuable time?**

Sharing your thoughts about the book through a review would be immensely appreciated. Your review serves as a beacon, guiding other readers to take a chance on my books. It's a small gesture that carries significant weight in the world of authors.

To submit your review effortlessly, please click on the link below. It will take you directly to the book's review page:

# "THE EVOLUTION OF BREATH"

Alternatively, you can also find the "**Reviews Section**" of this book's page on Amazon.

Your review will require just a minute of your time but will make a monumental difference in helping me connect with a broader audience and I eagerly look forward to reading your review.

Once again, thank you for your unwavering support of my work.

# DISCLAIMER

This book is for educational purposes only. Readers acknowledge that the author does not render legal, financial, medical, or professional advice. The content within this book has been derived from various sources. Please consult a licensed professional before attempting any techniques outlined in this book.

By reading this document, the reader agrees that under no circumstances is the author responsible for any direct or indirect losses incurred as a result of the use of the information contained within this document, including but not limited to errors, omissions, or inaccuracies.

Adherence to all applicable laws and regulations, including international, federal, state, and local governing professional licensing, business practices, advertising, and all other jurisdictions, is the sole responsibility of the purchaser or reader.

Neither the author nor the publisher assumes any responsibility or liability whatsoever on behalf of the purchaser or reader of these materials. Any perceived slight of any individual or organization is purely unintentional.

9 7 9 8 8 9 5 5 6 7 5 9 3